Parrots' Wood

The Peacocks of Baboquivari

Parrots' Wood

ERMA J. FISK

W · W · NORTON & COMPANY · NEW YORK · LONDON

Copyright © 1985 by Manomet Bird Observatory
All rights reserved.
Published simultaneously in Canada by Penguin
Books Canada Ltd, 2801 John Street, Markham,
Ontario L3R 1B4.
Printed in the United States of America.

The quote on page 175 is from the sonnet "Not in a silver casket cool
with pearls" by Edna St. Vincent Millay, from *Collected Poems,* Harper
and Row, copyright 1931, 1958, by Edna St. Vincent Millay and Norma
Millay Ellis. Reprinted by permission of Norma Millay Ellis.

The text of this book is composed in Garamond, with
display type set in Cochin Italic.
Manufacturing by The Maple-Vail Book Manufacturing Group.
Book design by Antonina Krass

Library of Congress Cataloging in Publication Data

Fisk, Erma J.
Parrots' wood.

1. Birds—Belize.   2. Belize—Description and travel.
3. Fisk, Erma J.   I. Title.
QL687.B45F57   1985   598.297282   84–29462

ISBN 0-393-01997-7

W. W. Norton & Company, Inc.
500 Fifth Avenue, New York, N.Y. 10110
W. W. Norton & Company Ltd.
37 Great Russell Street, London WC1B 3NU

2   3   4   5   6   7   8   9 0

For Jim.

You said once you were always looking for a book you could pull out of someone, even at cocktail parties. We were at a cocktail party.

Jonnie

"Adventure is just a state of mind, and a very pleasant one, and no harm to anybody, and a great asset if you use it right," wrote Archie Carr in a book I picked up at Washington International Airport in 1958. The book was *The Windward Road* (Knopf, 1956), an account of the adventures of a young biologist on the coastal beaches of the Gulf of Mexico. It changed my life, as the stories he recounts changed his. Dr. Carr went on to shape the thinking of two generations and of several countries in their regard for the importance of the wildlife resources of our planet. I—just went on, but my thinking was never again the same. I owe a great debt to Archie, whose wife and son I have met but who himself has eluded me. With this book I thank him.

Foreword

The occupations and names of some of the people in this book may be recognizable to some readers. However, all we know of our friends, even of our families, are the bits and pieces in our vision that revolve like shapes in a kaleidoscope, changing, blending, realigning with each pressure of our fingers, with circumstances, emotions, attitudes, age. What I discern in people is not what another, or a reader, might discern, nor what people themselves see in themselves. It bears no relation to Reality (if there is such a thing). So I consider that all the characters in this book are figments of my imagination. Including myself.

I thank those who have wandered in and out of my pages for their companionship, and the shifting colors with which they have illumined my passage. If they should occasionally recognize an incident in which they have participated, they will also recognize the fiction. I trust they will be amused rather than offended.

Introduction

What I remember in my life are its adventures, however small. When what I was doing became commonplace, when I knew that again I would be having a poached egg for breakfast, I was ready for a change. Well, usually. Those years with Brad may have been humdrum repetitions of the daily round, but they were so full of love and happiness that I felt no need for adventure. Besides, we had three children—no need to look outside our home for disruption of routine!

I never think ahead to what I may be getting into—a bus that doesn't make a hairpin turn in South America, the vagaries of weather and companions, dysentery, boredom. That's a funny word, whoever heard of boredom? Warm, comfortable, I launch myself out into chiggers, discomfort, food I wouldn't tolerate at home. I never consider a possible dark side to the coin. Not until too late do I wonder, Why Have I Done This to Myself? I have a granddaughter who is the same, I am severely critical of her. She will go anywhere, do anything at the drop of a suggestion. Irresponsible, I call it. In her.

The following journal—I guess you might call it that—is an account (well, something of an account) of a February I

11

spent on a hundred-acre plantation in Belize. Belize is the country in Central America that used to be called British Honduras. It's the size of Massachusetts, about, with the second largest barrier reef in the world, only 8 towns of any size, 200 inches of rainfall a year, 30 species of orchids, 6 or 7 of parrots, fewer than 150,000 people until refugees from Guatemala, El Salvador, Nicaragua started flooding across its borders. People don't seem to notice it on the map. The Guatemalans wish they wouldn't; they keep trying to absorb it for themselves. The former British owners have stayed on to defeat them.

I went there on a month's ornithological study. Not alone, as I have been three times in Arizona for The Nature Conservancy; there were a dozen of us mostly, people came and went. My account deals with no high adventure, just the minutiae of our weeks. It is the attitude, as Archie said, that counts. And my account is larded—any housewife my age knows what lard is—my account is larded with memories.

That's because at my age, memories, sounds, scenes, minutiae (what a useful word) swarm in my mind like bees about an apple tree, giving color, imparting fragrance and depth to what I am doing at the moment. Maybe this happens only to older people? The minds of the young teem only with the hopes, ambitions, whatever is accumulating at the moment that they will go back to years later? Do memories flood more strongly when you are on vacation, relaxed, divorced from the habits of daily routine? I don't know.

We are told we have two sides to our brain—one factual, logical, keeping us on track and knowing when dinner should be ready (and what to buy for dinner). The other creative, lacking a sense of time, wandering in a nonverbal world we too often neglect, a world of meditation and adventures (however small). I wander—if you haven't noticed you will shortly—

happily in both worlds. The only time it inconveniences me is when I am driving a car and seeing instead of traffic signs, Arizona mountains, seals bobbing in Pacific surf, myself hunting for the croup kettle in the attic and finding instead a chest of letters. While describing one of these or something similar to a passenger I am delivering to an airport, I forget to turn off the highway. If this kind of wandering inconveniences you, you shouldn't be reading this book.

Memories, that's what we were discussing. I don't know about you. I just know that my own life is lived in a tapestry of what has gone before, the unhappinesses blotted out by dog hair on the sofa, a child practicing on a violin, the trail of a train whistle across a night sky. You see what I mean? So that no matter what my present state, unless I am deeply concentrated (like trying at this moment neatly to type these pages so an editor can read them) I am moved and held upright by my past. Each moment is enriched by the minutiae (ah, again; WHAT a useful word, though I have a hard time spelling it and I'm not sure I can pronounce it).

"We overlook," writes Dorothy Gilman, author of the Mrs. Pollifax mysteries that delight me, in a journal I am reading, "how much in our lives is invisible; love, for instance; thought, God, the future, time, faith, hope and even the electricity that brings us light."

My memories are invisible, unknown to anyone but me. But unlike love and faith, a future that may not even exist, they are as real as these keys under my fingers, as the color and fragrance of this bowl of freesia and jonquils on my table.

Parrots' Wood

The Day Before

That was a pretty long introduction. I'm sorry. I'll try to remember to tell you later what I will be doing in Belize. At the moment I am lying on the cold cement floor of my Cape Cod, Massachusetts basement, wondering if I have broken a kneecap.

The trouble with accidents is that they are so sudden; no time to prepare. Once in a lifetime hasn't everyone the right to trip over an obstacle at the foot of stairs? Not, my Rational Self points out dryly, just before taking off for Central America on a research expedition.

Tentatively I flex my leg, decide to lie still a little longer. It may be better to contemplate my past than my future.

This is not the knee I scraped in Central America last year that brought me home in an airport wheelchair. It's the other one, the one I damaged in Texas once, tripping over a motel traffic bump when I was counting birds at a martin house. If you are a birder you look up, not down. I had spent that spring in the back seat of a small Cessna, surrounded by luggage, on an Audubon waterbird survey. We had flown from the Florida Keys around the Gulf of Mexico to Belize. As the only work I had to do was to peel oranges for the two men talking into recorders in the front seats, none of us had been inconvenienced by my mishap.

Am I accident-prone? Or have I just had so many years to accumulate scars? This one, below my kneecap, is from a palm stalk that slashed me when I was guiding a TV crew through vegetation on Grand Cayman, carelessly, showing off. I had had to come home. The one below that is from a rusty fence; one autumn I was greedily picking grapes and reached too far. I should have left them for the migrant catbirds I was studying. Although as I fell in love with the handsome young surgeon on duty that day in the hospital Emergency Room, and he rather with me, I didn't too much mind the necessary period of convalescence, with my foot up on pillows. He restored my happiness as well as my health, three of my grandchildren arrived to care for me, the whole interlude proved pleasant. Catbirds can be studied anytime, they are abundant.

I will skip the morning in Florida when I was leaving to collect orchids in Nicaragua. Unwilling to close my bird nets when I should have, hurrying, I fell on the rough limestone, clutching in either hand a Black-throated blue warbler and a Parula. The birds were undamaged. The branches of the small orange trees I had planted glistened above me in the hot light, against the blue of my Florida sky as I lay there on my back, my leg twisted, clutching those two small birds. When you live alone there is no one to laugh at you.

There is no one to laugh at me here, sprawled among the clothes I had been carrying for the cleaner and the mail that had spilled from my hands. It takes love to laugh. My children or my neighbors would frown, be critical of my lack of planning, my haste. Brad would have laughed, his anxiety concealed by an understanding of my lack of order.

None of these accidents were serious. What would I have done if they were? After Brad—went, I had to take care of myself. Some power through the years has guarded me. Or are our accidents, like our death, written in the stars? Programmed in our genes? All I know is to get through each the best I can, being cheerful. It isn't hard to be cheerful. You can fake it when you have to. Down in Florida when no friend arrived at my door I could chat with the garbagemen come to wrestle out my cans, with the postman in his motorized cart. (No such amenities on Cape Cod when you must drive to the dump and to the post office). They seemed pleased to be cheerfully greeted.

If I were really lonely in those days I could drive up to the University of Miami. Probably the young biologists at the Bird Range often faked their cheerful greetings too. They had many more problems than I, with their finances, their girls, third-hand cars, scholastic difficulties. I think it's when you don't have enough to do that you feel sorry for yourself. So I had better get up off the cement floor of my basement. I have plenty to do before I leave for Belize.

You see what I mean about living with memories? Those birds, those friendly students were seventeen years ago; or only yesterday. If you think I am just typing here at my New England window, looking out at snow and chickadees on my feeders, you are mistaken. My mind is jumping around in a dozen different countries.

Let's return to my basement, where again, and again tentatively, I flex my knee. I didn't land directly on the cap, perhaps it is only bruised. I pull toward me the scatter of packages, the laundry I had been carrying that had obscured my view, and pile them neatly. Always the housewife. With the help of a trash can I pull myself to my feet. My knee objects, but not too seriously. Good. No one would have come looking for me. No window or door looks in at where I fell. My family and friends know I am leaving, but I am always vague about my departures, needing a day of privacy for chores and packing. They thought I went off yesterday. I limp a few steps and glare at the cage of hardware cloth that had tripped me. Its frame is bent, I hit it hard.

It is human to blame someone else for your errors. This accident, I tell myself, is the fault of my editor in that New York publishing company. He had not understood, in the manuscript that has been going back and forth between us all winter like a frisbee, my reference to a balchatri trap. A balchatri is a device to catch hawks. This is not the place to explain my catching hawks, buy my book, *The Peacocks of Baboquivari.* (Since the royalties will go to The Nature Conservancy your money won't be wasted.) I was taking this trap to my illustrator to sketch. That is, I had intended to. The telephone rang, I set the trap down and neglected to return for it.

A few hours later, limping, I am packed. I have dealt with all urgent papers on my desk, wound the clocks (I always do) and am ready to leave. Astonishing. The telephone rings. It is my pleasant editor calling to wish me *Feliz viaje.* Only, social pleasantries over—

"I don't wish to shake you up, Mrs. F., but your manuscript hasn't arrived. When did you say you mailed it? And how?"

WHAT??? A week ago, more, for the last time I had sat up night after night reviewing his final comments, struggling with printers' language foreign to me, thanking a copy editor for catching egregious errors in my figures, scrawling aggravated notes where her changes irked me, laughing at generation gaps between us; explaining, polishing sentences. . . . Is it possible to read a manuscript even for the seventh time without feeling the need to alter it? Finished at last, secure in the knowledge that any problems were no longer mine, I had carefully wrapped that packet of sheets and dispatched it.

"How carefully?" pressed the voice on the telephone. "By what type of mail? Priority? Express? Did you insure it? Do you have a carbon, a meticulous carbon, that can be substituted?"

Naturally I fall apart. I have a faulty memory. I am always in a state of confusion when I am going away. I think I had boxed those sheets, but how had I wrapped the box? How had I labeled it? How am I to remember what I did a week ago? Mailing that manuscript has become as automatic as turning off the coffee pot. Of course I have a carbon, but not meticulous. It is marked up, scrawled over. No editor, however friendly, would work with it.

After he hangs up I dig out that carbon, discard it in dismay. Unless St. Anthony, patron saint of those who lose things, my staunch friend over the years, comes to our aid I will have to return from Belize.

I run down the lane to my family, who thought me gone. I instruct them on how to reach my publisher, how—possibly— they then might get in touch with me. I have been given two telephone numbers that should (but may not, Belize is not modern) reach one or the other manager of the two hotels in Belize City. If a message should reach one it will—it *should*— be relayed by a radio to a neighbor who lives a few miles from Dora Weyer's plantation, Parrots' Wood. If—IF—this neighbor is home to receive it sooner or later she will—she may— deliver it.

Having lived where communication was even less certain than this, then I tell myself to stop worrying, hug my grandchildren, go out for a Farewell Dinner.

I have told you, haven't I? Somewhere? That I am going to Belize on an ornithological expedition? Our group of twelve— there will be additions and deletions as the month wears on— is brought together by a research organization, the Manomet

Bird Observatory, of which I am a Trustee. I've been connected with the Observatory since the day it opened, only I splashed too much rum into the celebratory birthday punch bowl (it was my own birthday, too), so our connection came close to ending right then and there.

In the words of a letter that alerted us to this expedition, our purpose is to study one of the more accessible barometers of change in the biological world, the songbirds Passeriformes. These are easy to see, the letter mistakenly claims. They sing on territory during breeding season, so they can be easily located. (Huh! Among those tall, thick, leafy, hardwood forest trees?) They are sensitive to environmental stress and disaster. Their populations are relatively easy to monitor. They can be studied in the hand by the use of mist nets. Their age, sex, molt, the ectoparasites they may carry (don't cringe; these don't like humans), their condition noted. We would deal largely with birds of the forest and scrub, and with U. S. migrants. With the use of numbered and colored leg bands a biologist can mark the birds he handles, so that if one is recaptured its migration path can be traced, any changes noted, length of life determined.

Passeriformes is Latin for *sharp claws,* but birds will not hurt you. Whoever wrote this letter had not experienced pelican, whose toenails are indeed sharp, and have often scarred my wrists; nor hawks, which have given me puncture wounds. Neither of these, though, are songbirds. I would like to introduce the author of this informative and persuasive letter to a tropical Great Antshrike, *taraba major,* either male or female, a Passeriformes, family *Formicariidae,* definitely formidable. I wasn't permanently injured by one but my memories are crisp as its bill edges. You do not get mites, ticks, or lice from handling birds, nor diseases. I do wonder sometimes about the beards men tend to grow on field expeditions where water and mirrors are in short supply. There is a flat, blood-sucking fly, a hippoboscid, which inhabits the feathers of some bird species. When disturbed by our fingers, a luxuriant beard bending close to their host must present considerable temptation.

We would be studying particularly the interaction in food-seeking and habitat of the New World migrants—warblers, thrush, flycatchers and others that move back and forth from the tropics to our north. We are interested in the timing of their prebreeding molt, if any. If our investigations prove fruitful perhaps we can return to our study location on Dora's acres year after year, amassing useful information.

This gives you, I trust in reasonably understandable language, our mission. We will collect data partly by observation, partly by catching both local resident birds and the migrant North American species (and those shrikes) in mist nets. I'll tell you about mist nets shortly, stay with me. It's hard to get all this in at once. We will be properly specific, scientific about in what habitats—pine-oak or hardwood or gallery forests, scrub savanna, grassland, disturbed scrub—and at what levels the various species forage, who defends what size territories. We will be up early, so early to bed; share quarters. There will be "quarters"—roofs and beds instead of tents or platforms, showers instead of streams. We will be well fed—hooray! (Often I haven't been.) There will even be electricity. Well, of a sort. You know how generators are, particularly sixty miles from service. Compared to facilities I have cheerfully made do with this sounds the height of luxury. Our interests will be interrelated, so the companionship should be congenial.

As nothing in actuality is ever quite as anticipated, you must remember that Adventure is a State of Mind. Sometimes in the pages that follow I forget.

Day 1. Early morning

A gray, lowering, late January day. I am lowering too. I stayed too late at last night's party? Somewhere in my subconscious a warning stirs? I should be joyful, setting off on an adventure. I am too hurried to wonder about the implications of this, for as usual I am late. Munching a piece of toast I look about my living room with its many big windows—more of a bird blind than a room, my nonbirding friends tell me, laughing.

"Keep cool," I bid it. "Wait for me." I always wonder if I will get to come back to it.

Twenty-five miles north I catch the small plane that will ferry me to Boston. "Catch" is an old-fashioned word for the orderly filing by numbered boarding passes through carpeted corridors that lead you onto today's huge buses of the air. It still applies to a small-town airport when you arrive tardily, have to run out on the field with the ticket agent in the hope the pilot will see you and let down the steps of his small vehicle.

I am starting for Belize, a country in Central America. I told you this so long ago I'd better mention it again. Sleepy, but well ahead of time at Boston's Logan Airport, I buy a chocolate bar, a whodunit to pass the time, scrub my mind vacation-clean. While I am in the LADIES (only these days they call it less elegantly WOMEN, and graph a triangular skirt on the door. Don't complain, Mrs. Fisk, you've often been where a bush was all there was. Count your blessings) I hear my name urgently called. I react with alarm. My connections are tight. Our group is to meet in Belize City. From there we will be transported, I don't know how. By small plane? Airboat? Decrepit truck? I've used them all in that country. Sixty miles inland the dozen of us—biologists, volunteers, some with training, some enthusiastic tyros—will settle in for a week, two weeks, in my case a month of study. I know I keep repeating. Please ignore it. Don't I tell you something new each time?

I join an equally alarmed huddle at the reservation desk. All of us are tight-lipped. I storm at myself. *"What are you doing here?* Why are you always getting yourself into these situations? Last year you *promised* yourself you would never go south of Carolina again, don't you remember? This year you can't even get out of Boston!"

"Why are you going to that funny little country again?" friends had asked a few nights ago. If I were going to London or Vienna they would understand. Nice people. I enjoy the contrasts they offer to the woman I have become, widowed. They disapprove of the way I live, scold me, are sincerely troubled when I elect to stay in remote areas miles from help, from conveniences. Helen tries to keep me properly social, invites men she considers suitable to have dinner with me. Joe knows better.

"What would Brad say?" Helen asked, fretting. Suppose something happens to you, like last year? What medical supplies do you carry, will there be a doctor in your group?"

I had laughed. Neither of the two doctors on my last trip to Belize had even had a Band-aid with them. A scraped knee had become infected, brought me home finally in an airport wheelchair.

I hugged Helen affectionately, selected another of her decorative hors d'oeuvres, accepted another glass of wine from Joe. I wouldn't look at the picture of Brad they had conjured up, sitting in one of their comfortable chairs as he so often had, in their pleasant living room. That part of my life is gone. I try to look now only at whatever project I have managed to get involved in, which some researcher has offered, which will lead me away from that life. But it isn't easy.

I had walked to the windows to hide my face, stood with my back to them, sipping my wine. Turning—

"Don't you two scold me," I begged them. "I need you. I know I'm crazy. I suppose it's not knowing what I am getting into that attracts me, really—having to cope when I find myself in jams. So far I've been lucky. You would hate the discomforts, often the food" (Helen winced), "but I don't mind. The people are interesting, someone always takes care of me. I must look helpless . . ."

"Orders up a wheelchair for you?" Helen asked sarcastically. "Gets you a bed in that Boston hospital?"

I had prowled their room, restless. Unexpectedly, we had reached a deeper level. Their concern, the wine had broken through the tautness that sustains me. We were all aware of Brad, his presence in that big wing chair. Listening also, wanting to help me.

"I have to try things that are too hard for me. I don't have many friends left from the old days who put up with me the way you do; I've moved too far away, geographically and otherwise. I live in two worlds, not comfortable in either. I don't know where I belong."

Joe offered to refill my glass, but I shook my head. I was trying to think.

"Here with you I am comforted, coddled. Out with those researchers who use me I am an amateur, not yet at ease. It's like living on a seesaw. I have to learn to balance in the middle. I don't know where—or who—I am. I'm someone I have yet to define. Is this too much for you?"

This time, passing, I let my glass be refilled. The sound poured clear in our silence. Their faces were turned up in understanding.

"I've no one to straighten out my values. When you live in a family they let you know. Every day! They criticize you, tease you, love you. Tell you what you are doing wrong—or right. You have a man to do your thinking, open the mayonnaise jars, find your misplaced keys, slap you into bed at night.

"Now I have to make all the decisions. How do I know if they are right? Should I stay here, having friends for lunch, reading, hiring a neighbor boy to shovel the snow? Shovel it myself for exercise? Or do I launch myself out into chiggers, discomfort, food I wouldn't tolerate at home? Do I pick safety because I'm older now, or adventure?

"I work with men in their thirties and forties. They live in a different world than we do. They grew up during Vietnam, during the protests, the sexual and women's revolutions of the sixties. If I want them to like me, to earn their respect, I must adjust to attitudes very different from ours. It is a challenge. It keeps me on an edge. This trip to Belize will be easy. The group is mixed, I don't have to worry about being older. I've been there five times, I'll know more than most of them.

"I come back to you each time for TLC. I know I can count on you. You scold me—I love it—but you never let my seesaw down with a thump into the mud of my new playgrounds. There are plenty of others to do that—you had a few of them here this afternoon—Ted, Mary. . . . When *you* say something I can trust you. We all live on bases of shifting sands, need trust.

"You didn't understand that article I'd written." They laugh. "But that scientist you asked to meet me did. He knew what it means to an amateur to be published in such a journal. When someone of his stature says what he did to me I put it under my pillow nights, tresaure it until it is worn threadbare. Praise from the others, like Ted, is just fluff, cotton candy."

At the moment, standing at a reservation desk in Logan Airport on this raw, gray, winter day, even a handful of cotton candy caught on my coat would comfort me.

A harried young official tries to soothe us. Our plane is grounded in Providence. We will be accommodated by another line, if we can get to it in time. He herds us to a bus where— equally soothing—I sight my luggage wedged on a cart. I don't travel with much, and after experiences we won't go into I am careful always to carry in hand my binoculars, sneakers, tooth brush, notebooks. But I need what I take.

The bus is held up in traffic. My anxiety is compounded by a meager breakfast gulped long ago, before reaching that small plane that brought me to Boston. But all goes well, we are delivered in time, led aboard, a motherly seatmate shows me my seat belt, my flotation pillow. I told you I look helpless. (How many countries did Brad and I fly to after he retired into the Commerce Department? Forty-one? And how many have I been in since, on my own?) I thank my new friend. While I eat every scrap of breakfast that arrives, in case of no lunch, she pulls a ball of virulent green wool from her knitting bag and casts on stitches. A sweater for her latest grandson, she informs me proudly, and tells me how cute he and his brothers are.

I settle myself for sleep, only I don't sleep. In my handbag is an appeal for help, for advice, from a close friend who has remarried. No one really desires advice, but we all need— crave—support, reach blindly for it. I must figure out an answer to her.

"You seem to have conquered loneliness without remarrying," she writes. "How did you do it? I love Harvey but I find I am always tripping over him. He doesn't like it any better than I do."

Her situation doesn't take much pondering. I see it, or have it brought to me often—widows or widowers remarrying in their fifties and sixties. They start out radiantly happy. Lights are lit in their rooms at dusk, fine smells come from flowers in what had been an empty living room, from dinner cooking in the kitchen, no matter which of them may be stirring the skillet. They have defeated loneliness. But when the euphoria wears off they may find they have too much of a good thing. They trip over each other, as she says. They have lost, unless they are wise, a necessary degree of solitude.

Loneliness is an emotional state. Loneliness is when you have no one to bounce yourself off of, to recount the day's small activities to. A cat or a dog to pet and talk to can ameliorate loneliness. Solitude is different. If a marriage is to be successful each must have, or develop, a space of his own, for separate activities. Some men—I'm talking about retired ones, that's my age group, the ones I see—find it playing golf or shuffleboard, depending on their status. They build a greenhouse, do community work, keep a finger in business, go to a club for lunch. The women volunteer in nonprofit organizations, join reading or craft or church or garden groups, classes. They buy a loom, or an easel, turn a child's room into a studio, raise goats, breed dogs. The successful ones adjust, they have been through the mill. Each of the pair creates a space for dreams, for their own decisions, for solitude.

The younger ones have a lesser chance, they are more restive. They may divorce again or may build a sturdy relationship. The lucky latter, in the words of my Vermont aunt, settle into harness. Even in a good marriage you are restricted, life is a tradeoff, you can't have everything. But you can count on someone beside you to help pull the load, lending strength when the road is rough. You have a warm shoulder within touch, and that's mighty important.

People expect me to be able to give advice about loneliness because I have lived so much alone, in remote areas. I didn't know I was lonely, I was too busy coping. I had elected my solitude. My loneliness comes when there are people all about me but there is no one to whom I belong. That, maybe, is the core of successful marriage, to belong of your own volition. It is a choice you make, you and your partner. It takes care though, not to suffocate each other. You have to create a space about you.

How can I say this to my friend? Isn't it something everyone knows? Does she need to be told? She is looking for someone to bounce off of. Oh dear.

I pull out the whodunit I bought and lay it on my lap. But instead of reading I look out at the expanse of ruffled clouds below my window, wondering how I happen to be here. How do we choose a second marriage, a scientific expedition? What dictates the road we take? Robert Frost asked this question in a poem that haunts me. He was hesitating in a wood before two roads, a choice that he saw as making all the difference in life. Which urge is stronger, the known or the unknown? Well-worn ruts or a stream that may prove too shallow for the canoe, an alley in a foreign city leading where? If your road is—as mine was for many years—wholly satisfactory, such hesitation is pure greed. But who isn't greedy?

I have given myself over to the lift and sway of our ship. I love planes. (Or did before the seats became smaller and tighter, as I have become larger.) Someone else does the driving, pours the coffee, serves the meals, hands me a napkin, offers a magazine. I can become as excited as I used to be fifty years ago when on a voyage through the sea of air, lifting, swelling to a crest, gliding down—planes were smaller, more responsive to air waves then—you were aware how thin the metal skin was between you and the winds that roved the skies. Outside my window would tower a shifting wilderness of shadowed canyons, changing pinnacles of gleaming white, sunlit glory, threatening depths. Suddenly, frighteningly, a jagged mountain peak—this would be in Peru, where the pilots threaded their way adventurously through continental ranges; suddenly a forever expanse of ocean where miniature boats sailed on a frozen sapphire surface; or the random tracks of ancient rivers marked geological ages of our own country. An infinitude of space below me.

My first flights were two-dollar barnstorming ones from a grassy airfield in Buffalo, while the three men of my family, aged four through twenty-five, watched nervously from below. My first transcontinental flight was to Seattle as representative to a Junior League Convention. On the way we were attacked by thunderstorms. The plane pitched and moaned, as did the passengers, except for an interested man who helped me toss airsick bags along the rows, the stewardesses having cravenly strapped themselves into their seats. Lightning exploded on either side of us. I thought all flying was like this, a war with the elements to end, as that one ultimately did, in a calm and rainwashed sunset, the slopes of the Rockies instead of thunderbolts flaming below us.

On my return I came to a choice of roads. My seatmate was

a man of my own age, attractive, impeccable in clothes that spoke more of ranches than of cities. He recognized me by the sweeping black pirate hat that had marked me in a newspaper line-up splashed on the front page of the newspaper the day of our arrival. (We were displaced, the next day, by Hitler's invasion of Holland.) Finding that my acquaintance with western life derived only from Zane Grey, he urged me to break my journey at his stop of Pendleton, to spend a few days on an authentic western spread. He was open, friendly. His eyes twinkled as he sensed the shock of this proposition to my New England upbringing. He had a sister, he offered; she would chaperone us. It would be a shame for me to return east (he did not consider Buffalo west as I did, having been raised in Boston) untutored in what our country had to offer. He could provide a gentle riding horse. Why not?

I was sorely tempted. How easy it must be for women whose love is not securely rooted, who are not anticipating the welcome, the man who will be waiting, to slip briefly from the commitments of marriage, to forget or ignore the promises they made before the stresses of daily life obliterated these. As our plane refueled we walked along the chain link fence, he outside, me within. A desert wind lifted the wide brim of my hat. The land stretched limitlessly in beauty behind him. I was sure I wouldn't change my mind, he teased? What about those two small boys, I countered, running about at the airport gate, their father? My fingers and his eyes went to the flowers pinned on my shoulder, fragrant and visible sign of the love awaiting me. We parted with mutual regret.

But you see I still remember. Over all the years the temptation, the beckon of that other road has not faded. I wonder if he is now one of those cattlemen overgrazing the land I am always trying to save?

Long ago. Perhaps it is the happiness reflected in my face that catches the eye of a man balancing his way down the aisle of this plane forty years later. He stops to chat over the head of my seatmate. Considering me her private property she sniffs, then accepts the situation. When this new friend passes, the Atlantic is obscured by gray wool, our ship drones on flatly. I am shortly asleep. The whodunit can wait.

I awake to peanuts and orange juice, to the serene blue skies, the blue sea off Florida. We circle far out across the Everglades, where I used to be flown in a little Park Service plane to make surveys of eagle nests, of thousands of the wading birds that existed then, of rafts of white pelican, duck, coot. We circle over the square-mile agricultural fields about Homestead, which provide winter tomatoes and potatoes and beans and mangoes and limes and huge avocados for the nation's dinner tables. Being displaced how—the fields, not the tables, which may some day be bare as fields—by square miles of trailer parks and condominiums.

A friend used to keep me in two-pound avocados from her dooryard tree—delicious, rich, each one lasting me a week, I didn't count the calories. I lived for twelve years in Homestead, eight months of the year in a farm cottage on a former tomato field rented to me for $1,000 a year on a lifetime rental! That was before Miami had entirely become the megalopolis tied up in ribboned highways that now stretches from Palm Beach to Key Largo, and down across turquoise-lapped bridges to Key West. Life changes, interests shift, friends move away. Progress and bulldozers thinned the bird life I had studied. My cottage was robbed, vandalized, robbed a second and third time. The police were insistent I blank out the soft nights, replace the moon that lit my windows with spotlights. My friends wanted me to carry a gun, to have guard dogs. I left

Florida. I don't miss, now, that barefoot life I loved, going out at dawn to pick my breakfast from grapefruit trees I had planted myself, except for being able to be out of doors every day from moonset to moonrise.

I ate Christmas Dinner once, early on, with a man who told me how as a boy he used to row from Miami across to the Beach. There was nothing along the coastal edge then but mangrove and Jake's Place, where he could get a Coke. (If there was Coke in those days. He would have been too young for a beer.) He used to own miles of land where now a main route south bears his name; he said he could cry every time he drove it and saw the changes. I think of him, of the mangrove swamps and crocodiles and mosquitoes, of fishing boats along that sparkling strand as again we circle, this time over miles of interlaced highways, golf courses, and race tracks, polluted canal fingers, the bulldozer-maintained beaches, the shimmering distances of tract housing. Affluent, each with its swimming pool, but still tract houses. Palms instead of mangroves. No wood storks, no great flights of white ibis under our wings; the manatees, now an Endangered Species, now scarred by propellers of the boats cuddled up to every dock.

We swing in finally over busy boulevards where racial violence is commonplace, over the Perimeter Road where I used to park to birdwatch. I notice a lack of grackles and gulls on the grass between the airport runways. So the Port Authority has finally found a way to be rid of its animal life? In my day there had been jackrabbits and prairie dogs and other escaped fauna as well as birds, although these exotic hazards were not publicized. Somewhere inside by the central escalator used to be an Audubon plaque proclaiming the airport a sanctuary for burrowing owls. If it is still there it is not visible among the jostling lines of travelers, families spread out on the floor with babies and paper bags and stuffed animals and lunches. There can be no owls outside either in that jostle of international planes coming and going. Back when it was emptier the Miami Airport was my Club; I constantly encountered friends from past years. Once, unexpectedly at 3:00 A.M., my elder son and his wife—both of us setting forth on Christmas trips to Peru, but separately. Once, equally unexpectedly, my daughter. I hadn't known either of them would be there. As my son pointed out, do you write your mother that at 3:00 A.M. you will be changing planes at an airport thirty miles away, why doesn't she drive up and say Hello? I had to agree with him.

Our children! During those years, distant in Florida, the thought of them was like the bugling of geese skeining against my horizon in an affirmation of life, of continuity; like the half-remembered music of spring peepers when dusk settles among the trees of a swamp. Like the soft fall of snow outside a window reflecting firelight inside. Like music spilling through an open doorway, across a lawn I used to pass walking home at night. Only I couldn't listen to music in those days. It cut too deeply through the protective layers with which I struggled to mute my loneliness, into a quiet desperation that could seize me unawares.

I had separated myself from our children. I hadn't dismissed them, just set them aside until I had learned to stand by myself. It wasn't that I didn't still love them or, I suppose, they love me. At that stage of our lives they were building their own families. I was trying to build a life among people who didn't know if I had children, if there was a "Mrs." in front of the nickname they called me by. I was building with tools foreign to my hands, in a land and a culture strange to me.

I used to send the children my itinerary whenever I went out of the country, "in case they needed me." Later I realized

I was doing this not for their security but for my own. I was clutching, trying to find a place where I belonged, was needed. I couldn't emotionally accept that I wasn't. If I returned from Costa Rica they might call and ask cheerfully, "How was Trinidad?"

We visited back and forth. I still carry in my wallet a faded snapshot of our daughter, holding her own small daughter by the hand at the base of Everglades National Park. The heat had horrified them and the mosquitoes sent us early indoors as the sun slid behind the pines. A police officer in the North, displeased with my driving, saw this photograph once as I rummaged for my license to show him. He recognized the background of palms and Bay, became so nostalgic about a vacation he too had spent among those mosquitoes that he put away his pad of traffic tickets. We talked about the Miami Airport, where you can see nearly anything in behavior or costume.

"Never did see a dame wholly naked," he regretted, "but they sure came close to it! Wish we had weather like that up here."

At last our plane taxis in. At one extreme of the airport, I am to leave from the other. If it is not already too late. I am first in line to disembark—

"Run," bids my stewardess. "Don't worry about your luggage, it will get there before you do. But run!"

Why don't they send me perched on the dolly with my bags, I wonder? It would be quicker, easier. Hurt the airport image, I suppose. Start a trend.

"Don't run," my doctor has been telling me all winter. "Don't get excited."

I run. The Miami Airport has been home to me for too many years, it won't let me collapse with a heart attack today.

I can rest on that flight to Belize, which is further in sitting time than it looks on the map. How long had it taken Gene and Sandy and me to fly there from the Keys the year we made a wading bird survey around the Gulf of Mexico for National Audubon Society? We were in a little plane, a Cessna. As always we were grounded in Lafayette by rain. (Rain, rain, does the sun never shine in Lafayette? Not when I am there.) I hurt that knee, counting martins. The doctor's pills made me sleepy, I had slept the whole length of Padre Island, one of the famous bird spots I had wanted for years to see. We must have been a week and more reaching Belize, held up at each stop by Mexican officials who coveted our emergency supplies and our rifle Ah, that rifle! Gene would never tell me how much it cost in bribes to keep it. I guess you can't compare the trips. Even in a jet today's trip will be long, broken only by peanuts, the lunch and liquids stewards dispense to ease monotony and keep us in good humor.

Midway through the airport, panting, backpack askew, I am advised by a bulletin board that my departing plane has been delayed. So I pause, as always, to greet my husband where he had stood by the Pan Am desk on our last trip. After twenty years his presence still is there, in that green shirt and madras hat, his hazel eyes warm with affection, laughing at me; saying—Off again? Saying—I love you. I stand, heedless of the people that push around me. Slowly, eyes focused far away, I too push through the flow into a drugstore and concentrate on buying another whodunit, anodyne for sleepless nights. Then again I set off to meet the friends of my current life, with whom I am about to embark on this newest adventure.

Still Day 1

In Belize City the sun blazes, the air is incredibly humid. Waiting in line for Immigration we sweat in our travel clothes, but we don't mind, we are too excited by novelty. And where is my second suitcase, the canary-yellow one? In the belly of that plane that has just taken off for Venezuela in a chaos of noise and dust? Still in Miami?

The first lessons you learn in the tropics are patience, flexibility, how spoiled and expectant of organization North Americans, certainly urban North Americans, are. It is hard for us to roll with the punches. The first time I went anywhere alone after Brad died to see if I could handle traveling by myself, at 2:00 A.M. in a Mexican airport officials were unwilling to admit me. My luggage had not arrived, and as in a hotel, a female with no luggage had no respectability. As if it were *my* fault! Waiting patiently while bureaucracy wrangled, I had watched a United States executive type try to harass a porter into American—North American—efficiency.

"There is a man," I had remarked with amusement to a woman standing near me, "who is going to be miserable in this country."

"I know," she replied sadly. "He is my husband. He thinks this is Connecticut."

A month later we encountered each other in Uxmal. I was running a temperature of 102°F., allergic to pepper trees blooming luxuriantly in the hotel gardens. They cared for me, fed me rum lemonades, arranged my passage home. Our executive had grown less structured. They became, and still are, good friends.

In our group today we have a couple of executive types. What time will we arrive at Parrots' Wood? they want to know as our bags are piled into the van that has met us, into the back of our hostess Dora's station wagon. Will there be time to birdwatch before supper? Will the nets have been set up by those who arrived early? How many *are* already arrived?

Dora, hostess and guide for our group, a valued friend to me, is listening to the engine of her new car—just bought, she tells me proudly; only third-hand. It sounds a bit third-hand to me, as if it might need attention.

Her answers are vague. Parrots' Wood is inland some thirty miles, the ride will take two hours or more. Would we like to birdwatch along the way? Compare waterbirds of the river edge—the Belize River—with what we will find as the terrain changes? The slightest elevation gives a change in soil, and so a difference in habitat and species. Hawks and flycatchers will replace egret and heron. There is a cucumber field where we might see several hundred Fork-tailed flycatchers. It is off our route a bit, but well worth the extra distance. She turns to me for corroboration, she had taken me there one year. She and I both know it is the wrong season for Fork-tails and cucumbers, but she has distracted them; our passengers chirp away excitedly.

Dora is North American, efficient, with a sense of time, but she has lived long in tropical countries, been in Belize for twenty years. Breakdowns and unanticipated events bother her little. She and her daughter, Diane, are the naturalists of this undeveloped country, respected by and familiar with its governors. Specialists from the worlds of museums and zoos, the fields of photography, geology, ornithology, botany come constantly to their doors. They had written me of the recent acquisition of a hundred acres, wild, lumbered long ago, scarred by devastating fires, often flooded. These will be our base, a control area for what can become a long-term study of migrant birds on their wintering quarters, of the effects of the devastation of forests in tropical countries.

She has boundless enthusiasm, a rich voice, and deep love for her tropics, acquired from a background of years working in Africa with her husband, from the many natural history tours led through Central America that have supported her widowhood. We are old friends, she puts me in the front seat beside her. It is hard to keep her hands on the wheel. She uses them to point, to gesticulate, for emphasis. It is great fun to be back with her, living dangerously. Skillfully she deflects tensions, reminding me (for our passengers' benefit) of when we have seen this bird, where we hunted for that; branching off into stories, waving her hands, breaking into her deep laughter, stopping to run back along the road to tell the occupants of the van behind us what they should be seeing. She drives and stops, her running commentary never ceasing. A wealth of information spills over us.

The scenery is lush, and familiar to me, the air deliciously warm. I contrast with pleasure the comfort, the joy of all this with a similar scientific expedition I had taken last year. There our drive had been a long endurance test in a truck, hanging onto wooden benches. Luggage and food for our ten days were heaped behind us, our native helpers slid about on top of it. It had rained much of that miserable journey. If we fastened the canvas flaps our quarters became dark and viewless, although by standing we might peer through slits and tears, absorb the jounces with our knees instead of our backsides. When we raised the flaps light rain blew in, and a cold, rough wind. Why, I had wondered through the hours, does it always rain when I go to Central America in the dry season? Huddled and tired, I had envied the woman curled up against her husband's shoulder, his arm and jacket warming her. But then, I envy all women with an affectionate chest to lean against; it doesn't need a truck to bring out that emotion in me.

There is no rain on today's drive. Wedged together, contours of hips, thighs, feet, and occasionally, as someone turns, the softness of bosom, we will be well acquainted by the end of this drive. It is a good way to start an expedition that may later become less comfortable, assuring that we will, because we must, get along well together. We are a baker's dozen, middle-aged and older. Some have worked in the tropics before. Some are reputed figures in ornithology. Some will make up with sharp eyes and zest for a lack of technical knowledge, will learn to extricate birds from our nylon nets without losing a feather, to keep the records destined for computers. Some wish to amplify the lists of birds they have seen elsewhere. They plan to tramp the roads, not yet knowing the bush will be too thick to break through.

What people are shows clearly on trips away from their usual habitats. Well, not always clearly; we all put our best feet forward. But away from home we are like fish in an aquarium, a different light illumining our colors. I am aways curious about other people, disappointed if they prove dull or selfish. I want to like everyone, to learn what makes them tick; which, of course, I never can, really. How well do we know our roommates or friends, our parents, a spouse on the deeper levels where simmer emotions and motivations even they dislike to acknowledge? There is always a protective glass wall through which we glimpse only flashes of movement. Then we lose our quarry in a fountain of obscuring bubbles, a bed of ferns, the doors of a castle . . .

As she drives, Dora's voice encompasses us. She is an Earth

Mother—large, full-breasted, with an embracing warmth, a caring that searches out and smooths any problem. I have traveled with her many times, it is a delight. We don't always agree, but we always end up laughing. It is good to be back with her, good to be out of the raw, northern winter. In this country anything can happen. I capture her hand again and restore it to the wheel.

Does she still have her cages of snakes, of animals, that gorgeous, topaz-eyed shepherd dog that no one but herself dares handle? I ask.

No. This new plantation, Parrots' Wood, which was to be the support of her age, had almost immediately been ravaged; first by fire, then by hurricane. The orchards she had planted, the nurseries that were to make her fortune, were destroyed. Huge trees that had been passed over in the long-ago lumbering, too small to cut, had been torn out, twisted—we would see. Small streams that everywhere run in this sea-level land had turned into raging torrents, had flooded her grounds, drowned her animals. Her face shadows as she speaks of her disaster. She has had to start again, from nothing. Then she dismisses it with a wave of her hand, a humorous story of hearing her dogs cry in the night. Looking down—houses are built here on stilts for just such floods—she had seen them struggling, their heads strained up above rushing water. Knowing her love for animals I am aware that this had not been humorous, but she is laughing, she can turn anything into drama, into entertainment.

She rattles on as we travel, only from her it isn't "rattling." I marvel at the skill with which people—some people, I can't do it—handle their fellow men. Our group is a mixture of ages and interests, of reasons for being here. They are excited, tired, bewildered by their tropical surroundings. Left alone they might become morose, difficult, eye each other without pleasure. But Dora has them, even in two separate vehicles, melded, eager-eyed, enjoying each other. I watch her with admiration as well as affection. Are you born with this talent? Can it be taught? Why did I have to wait so long to see how important it is? I'm not talking about glibness, insincerity; to work it has to come from the heart, be a part of the heart. What molds us—our genes, accidents of our childhood, our parents? Success or failure among our peers? Could I learn at this late date not to be a loner, or am I programmed by now too rigidly? Do I want to try? That's what really directs us— the wanting. And maybe a willingness to accept defeat. Bit by bit, though, trying can inch us ahead.

We turn from the smooth new highway that runs across Belize to Guatemala onto its once proud predecessor, now crumbled and upheaved by ten years of rain. This is Dora's land. Maybe we will be willing to get out for a moment while the cars negotiate the sharp drop at the verge, cross the mud hole beyond? Just for a minute? No, we should not try to walk in, it is a mile to the gate. We must sort ourselves into our sleeping quarters before dark; there are only oil lamps for illumination.

And so at last, near dusk, we arrive. We unpack suitcases, backpacks, sunhats, cameras, telescopes, boots—what a lot of gear people can bring! We carry it off—men in one direction, with them one wife; the women to Diane's house, with us one husband who will have to accept females running up- and downstairs in their wrappers (or without) to the shower room. If he is modest he must learn to dress and undress rapidly in the dark.

With only one suitcase to carry I outdistance the others on our quarter-mile path. Through a gate that controls two guard dogs, through the former orchard, past a pond, over two small bridges—one of planks that must wash away in rain (always carry a flashlight); one curving high over its stream; up a little hill, through a low section, slipping in mud, through pine trees. Two water tanks by the house will catch rain from the roof. My practiced eye measures them. Not very big tanks— unless it rains, our personal showers had better be brief, jeans left muddy, city women forewarned. I've been through this before. City women, new to seasonal drought, feel a need to do laundry daily, leaving all of us waterless until they learn.

I mount the steps to the second floor, select a bed in the Ladies' Dormitory, a long, pleasant room gutted to accommodate us. A bookcase runs its length, well stocked. (Good.) No closet, no chairs. We can hang our clothing on the windows, they swing in. Very comfortable. (Immediately I crack my head on one.) Downstairs are beds for the married couple, a shower room. An outhouse is visible from the windows. Rain, we find as time passes, comes in onto beds if windows thoughtlessly are left open. You learn to be thoughtful early. A wet bed is inconvenient for sleeping, sitting, stacking clothes on.

After supper comes First Night Briefing. On the use of water, on meal hours, on the two Doberman dogs that protect us— Dora doesn't elaborate from what. The usual tropical warning of tropical rattlesnakes, big; coral snakes, small; the deadly fer-de-lance and others, all of which may be present on heat-holding paths at night, so we MUST use flashlights. I doodle, bored with talk of snakes. In all the tropical countries I have been and worked in I have encountered snakes only on open roads, usually dead. Although once, in Big Bend, Texas, walking with the president of the New York Zoological Society, we met a large rattlesnake sunning across our path. It observed the two of us—after all *we* were the invaders—then slithered between some rocks. As it disappeared it lifted the end of its tail and rattled disdainfully. Unless you surprise them, step on them, most snakes seem willing to get out of your way. Not the fer-de-lance. My eyes drop to Dora's ankle, but her slacks conceal the hideous scar I am told is there.

A four-letter word pulls me upright. CATS! Big Cats! They are common in this area; if we are lucky we may see their prints, here in her compound. ("Lucky" seems an odd choice of words.) A puma, a female puma, often pads back and forth between this Main House and Diane's, where we will live, its prints visible in the mud. With a three-quarter grown cub, also a female, they stay with their mothers for a year. They jump easily over the fences, drink from the pond. I can't contain my excitement. This is *true?* I ask Dora. She isn't fooling? A puma is a mountain lion, a cougar, a panther—it has many names. Every day in those mountain canyons in Arizona where I studied birds for The Nature Conservancy I trained my telescope on the slope with the prayer of seeing one. They were there, I found their prints by the Creek, and once, high by the base of a cliff, their trail through deep grass, but I never saw one.

Dora is pleased by my excitement. She had shown me a puma on a previous trip, in a backyard zoo. Refusing to accept captivity, it had padded, padded along its wire, ignoring us, its smoky eyes fixed on some unimaginable distance into its past, its long, dark-tipped tail ceaselessly twitching. I can't stand to see animals caged.

There are jaguars, too, Dora continues, so abundant they are considered a pest. They can kill a full-grown bull with one bite through its skull. They take dogs. (Not her Dobermans, I'll wager.) Their eyes shine green. Surprisingly, they are sometimes killed on the highway, like deer in our country. They must be abundant! Ocelots are spotted fawn and brown like the smaller margays. The latter have long whiskers, long legs out of proportion, eyes of deep amber. These aren't here, and the puma seem to have scared off the ocelots. Jaguarundi roam the forest about us though, drink also at night from our pond, are slim enough to push through the hogwire, or climb over the fences. Probably we will create too much disturbance to see them, although perhaps—in the full of the moon. . . . Around the table our eyes, blue, brown, gray, shine bright with anticipation.

We will know when the puma, the mountain lion, is around, Dora laughs. Its purr is more irritable than soothing, and it smells awful. No one told me that in Arizona. There the wind blows keen and dry over the slopes. Here in the humidity scent would linger in the air.

I sit, dreaming of cat eyes glittering through the underbrush, while Dora goes on to describe paca, agouti, the armadillo and opossum that come for the prolific yellow fruit of craboo. She tells of sounds that will be strange to us—the wooden clamor of *Bufo marinus,* a huge toad that excretes a poison from its glands and so cannot be eaten. It is in the grass along the fences; we will see it often. I already have. Sometimes their call is like the tremolo of a screech owl, I contribute. Some idiot brought them into the United States, loosed them in Miami, they have become a pest. They eat small birds, too. We shouldn't pick up the frogs, there is another with lovely golden eyes, some people are allergic to it.

The night call of the resident Great potoo resembles the scream of a woman being choked.

I slip out, hoping to smell a puma, reluctant to use my flashlight. Past the pond glimmering under stars, up to the room four of us will share, its wide windows open to the soft tropical night. I leave one of the two tiny oil lamps at the foot of the stairs to guide my companions, another at the head; light the candle in the shower room and am in bed before anyone arrives to join me. Tonight not even the grunts and purrs of a big cat outside are going to disturb my slumber. The sounds and clatter and crush of this day's three international airports are far away.

Day 2

Before we go any further I would like to explain a few things I take for granted, to orient you before you get impatient.

What I like to do is study birds—in the hand, rather than observing them in the bush tail-to, hidden behind leaves. No matter whether they are the Endangered pelican I used to try to tease within reach in Florida Bay, the feisty chickadees that peck my fingers on Cape Cod, or the iridescent hummingbirds that excite me from Peru—where there is a brown one the size of a robin, *Patagona gigas peruviana*—to Quebec where Ruby-throats came to a tube of sugar water held in my hand.

I was a housewife, very happily so, for thirty-six years. In three heart-stopping days I lost that portfolio. For a long while then I was nothing, a zombie. My children were married, scattered. I had no training. Friends advised me to go back to school, to use my willingness to talk as a teacher. (I love to talk, if there is a podium between me and my audience. No one can interrupt me.) I didn't want to go back to school, to be indoors, I like to be outside. Besides, I didn't expect to live much longer. That was twenty years ago. I didn't know how exciting life was going to become.

I did have a small hobby I had developed in midlife of handling birds, of bird banding. That is, of trapping resident birds in my back yard, and migrants that might feed in my shrubs spring and fall. I would put a numbered government ring on the leg of each to discover how long they lived, if they returned, for how many years. I studied what they ate, their plumages, learned if they moved about the neighborhood, how far; if they kept their mates. Sometimes I trapped birds not to be expected in the area, a matter of interest to ornithologists. I could do this, a little, between cooking and caring for my family. It upset them when I let the supper burn, or left the table to run out to liberate a woodpecker or a wood thrush from a trap, but they adjusted (slowly). They even adjusted (slowly) to the dead tree I insisted we leave standing when flickers, nuthatches, and chickadees took up residence in it. I took children's courses at our Science Museum.

As local ornithologists learned of my interest they trained me to be useful to them. This pleasantly replaced my serving on Mothers' Councils, the telephoning and fund-raising for organizations I had never really enjoyed. I began what might be called—politely—my lecturing career then too, talking about birds and conservation to the neighborhood Cub Scout groups. It's astonishing how much conservation you can work into a talk on how and what birds eat. And vice versa when your audiences expand, as mine have over the years, to adult groups— of any stripe, horticultural, political, civic—I take any of them on cheerfully and brazenly. Some of them even pay me for my pleasure. Groups are always looking for offbeat programs, so I am kept busy, as the cliché is. Widows must look for ways to keep busy, something has to get us up mornings. And keep us from taking naps afternoons. I'll get enough sleep when I'm dead.

Gradually I dabbled my way into amateur ornithology, After

Brad died this small hobby led me by degrees into nearly a full-time occupation, serving professionals who need willing arms and legs. That their projects were in Ecuador, Trinidad, Mexico, the coastal marshes of Maryland (mosquitoes!), the foggy spruces of Maine (black flies!) didn't deter me. They took me along because they needed extra help, however untrained, and my banding permit. They taught me. I was willing always to do things their way. Why not? I didn't know any other. I was full of enthusiasm and cheer. Why not? I was having a marvelous time. I slept soundly again at night. As a widow I was hungry for the companionship of men (there were few women professionals in those days). I wasn't hunting a husband. Even if I had been these men were fifteen, twenty, then thirty years younger than I. (These days it is forty and fifty, which horrifies me. It must horrify them often, too.) They took for granted, and still do, that I carry my own gear, climb in and out of their boats and trucks unassisted, wade streams, take care of myself (and them, bringing along gingerbread, cookies, suitable thermoses). In return they ran the boats and trucks, did the planning and thinking, warmed my loneliness with their friendship, gave me an occasional affectionate hug. Who could ask for more?

At home they brought me their girls to approve, and feed. I had to learn to accept the language and life-styles of generations very different from mine. A useful tolerance as my grandchildren grew through their teens. I acquired flexibility along with a knowledge of ornithology.

Living was usually uncomfortable, or at least different. At La Playa Escondida in Mexico I had to elbow my way through a herd of cattle and walk through muddy you-know-what to get to breakfast. Life like this keeps you from getting into a rut. Some places you may not even get breakfast. This is good for you, too. Each trip I took, whether a day, a month, or, as once in Arizona, an entire winter alone on a mountain, was an adventure.

Through my excursions I became drawn onto conservation Boards. We can't have birds in our world unless they have habitat, a place to live. There can't be habitat in these times of zooming population, of forests being destroyed, of chemicals poisoning the ground, of air and water pollution—all the craziness with which we are laying waste our planet—unless we fight for it. Just a few remnants of it. I'm not much at sitting about Board tables; I prefer to be out in the field. Maybe thirty years is a long enough span to indulge a hobby like bird banding. Maybe I should acknowledge that my joints creak, my ears and eyes are not what they were. Maybe I should now work at a desk instead of in a wilderness. But you notice where I am, don't you?

I don't know how my month on Dora's plantation in Belize will work out, but I'll bet it will be fun. I can already see it will be comfortable. No cows, no mountain miles to pack in supplies, no crocodiles. As the Group Elder I can probably do what I like, be active or lazy as I please. There are plenty to handle the work. Our experts have far more professional knowledge than I. I doubt there will be any High Adventure to record, just minutiae. It will be the attitude that counts, as Archie wrote.

Day 2 Continued

Breakfast is juice, eggs, thick slabs of local bread. No such luxury as toast, the advertised electricity is four low-watt bulbs strung in our Common Room. Diane brings platters of hot biscuits to the two long tables where we will eat, study, write our notes, sort laundry, and push aside the books always piled there.

We are given another briefing, this time on observations to put in notebooks handed to us. What North American migrants we identify, doing what, at what levels of vegetation? Eating, if we can determine this, what? Associating with what other species? Paired, as they would be in the north, or vigorously defending territory even from the opposite sex? We call them "our" birds, but they may spend seven months of the year in the tropics, coming north to breed, their arrivals timed for explosions of the insects best suited to their needs. A high-protein diet is necessary to breeding birds; insects are almost exclusively what is fed to nestlings. When the parental job is done the birds return to the tropics. There, if heavy rains or the long dry seasons of winter make insects scarce, species can change diet. Fruit eaters may switch to grain, to nectar, then back again. Their food, like ours, depends on what is available and abundant, or on their interaction with local residents. Behavior may change too, species solitary in the north joining in flocks. I was puzzled one fall on my own migration down the Atlantic coast to count forty-two Eastern kingbirds, which I know only as a solitary and highly pugnacious species, grouped like swallows along a utility wire—a flocking behavior they exhibit in their winter habitat. Any information we can garner, we are told, will be useful. That's a tall order for one month, with changing personnel! The faces around the room are eager. We write our names on our new notebooks.

The overall reason for our study, of course—I should manage to slide this in somewhere, we discuss it in one or another aspect constantly—is that as tropical forests are cleared for agriculture, for pasture to cater to the U. S. gluttony for hamburger, the number of birds dependent on forests for survival is declining steadily. Ornithological research documents this; we will contribute our mite. It is estimated that by the year 20,000 primary tropical forests with their wealth of medical, botanical, and wildlife resources for humankind will be gone. As some 75 percent of our wood warblers alone winter in Central America, this is a matter of great concern to ornithologists. Much concentrated study is under way.

While Trevor instructs us in the above I have been timing a small hummingbird—a Red-billed Azurecrown—on its forays to the calliandra bush just below me. It zooms out from a branch, snaps up some infinitesimal insect, returns to the exact twig it left from. I make the first entry in my notebook, then people start moving about, obstructing my vision. This afternoon, tomorrow, I will time it again, I have a month ahead of me for such play. I had better explain right now that anything I enjoy doing is play. Work is what I have to do, don't want to do, had better get behind me as fast as possible. And not scamp it as too often I tend to, or I will have to do it over.

We women return to our cottage for our cameras and gear, then make our way, getting lost, we live on the far side of the pond, do not yet know the paths to the men's quarters, which will be headquarters for today's activities.

The men's quarters turn out to be a shack. Sorry, Dora. Well, even Dora admits it is a bit of a shack, although it has sheltered some famous names. I understand—I thought it best not to go inside to look—that there are three small dark rooms, the beds edged with dufflebags, a sort of a shower in the corner of one. This is beyond the double bed the wife shares, so privacy may be a bit of a problem. Jaime, our boy of all works, is climbing up and down a rickety ladder, balancing a pail to fill the larger boiler propped on the roof that supplies this shower. Out in the field is a biffy, politely facing away. A handsome placard with a parrot painted on it—the gift of a modest guest—proclaims occupancy. We ladies purr at the luxury of the house we live in, recently built, with many windows. Perhaps we should invite that wife, in the midst of showering males, to trade with the one man in our harem? No, says our curious investigator, the rooms are so dark it doesn't matter. Also with a double bed the man involved might wish a say-so? We agree we are glad we are not resident here, just lowly unskilled labor standing about a card table, waiting to be assigned duties.

Beyond the open field, a wet ditch here and there, watch your footing, is high scrub. Scrub savanna is its official name. The men are setting up nets in it, stretching them three to six in a row as the terrain permits. Instructions are shouted back and forth, machetes are in use. Someone comes running to announce a Pygmy kingfisher sighted by a small stream. A Pygmy kingfisher is a charming bird, the size of a sparrow, with a rich mahogany chest, fine white spots on its wings, the heavy saw-edged kingfisher bill nearly as big as its body. It lives on small minnows and even what it may find in small mud puddles. As it is not common there is an immediate exodus, the tyros learning that you cannot hurry along narrow net lanes—feet, buttons on your clothing catch in the delicate nylon mesh. I sigh as I watch them extricate themselves. They will have left tears that need mending. I have bobbin and thread with me. The willingness to mend nets is one of my assets. Undisputed.

The net lanes have not yet been trampled down, I find, exploring them. I trip over logs, step in holes, catch my own clothing on the many brambles (but not on nets. I have thirty years' experience). Here a shirt has been discarded, there a water bottle hangs on a stub—it is already hot. I gather up such leavings, return them to our center, go off the other way, joining two of the men carrying a load of net poles. I am pressed into service to hold these, to string nets, to locate other lanes Jaime has cleared for us. Lost, I tear strips from the Kleenex in my pocket, tie them at the switchbacks. Until the next rain, until our feet have worn descriptive paths, these will get us back and forth.

Bird nets—I had better explain bird nets. Mist nets. I wrote a book—is that manuscript lost? *What am I to do if it is?? I'll have to go home. I worry, every hour.* I wrote a book about a winter I spent pretty much alone and incommunicado on a mountain in southwest Arizona, weathered in to everyone's dismay. I was doing a bird study for The Nature Conservancy. I didn't think to explain bird nets in my original manuscript, they being as common a tool in my work as the skillet in your kitchen (maybe you call it a frying pan). I had been brought up sharply on this omission by my editor, whose address is Fifth Avenue, New York, where I guess bird-banding nets aren't common. Since he is a perfectionist I had had to provide a meticulous, illustrated insert on mist nets. Maybe I should provide something here.

According to its label a mist net is 12 meters long by 2.6 high. That's about as long as a tennis net (I think). Anyway, the nets, stretched tautly from pole to pole, are in five tiers. They are fashioned so that when a bird mistakenly flies into one—birds have acute eyesight, my theory is they must be looking over their shoulders, or daydreaming to get caught. If a hole is available I have watched them fly right through it, not missing a wingbeat. If they fly into one, I am saying, their weight sags the nylon mesh and they drop below one of the

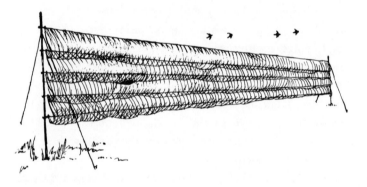

taut horizontal cords into a sort of pocket. Here, I'll give you a picture, there is no way I can describe this in words. If you throw a rock at material stretched tightly the rock bounces off, doesn't it? Birds do too. If a rock or a bird hits loose material it gets caught; nets are programmed for this. We catch enough birds to satisfy us.

You see, I can't stay away from words, but maybe this sketch will help.

No, of course I didn't draw it, we all have our limitations. I have a friend, Louise Russell, she did the illustrations for my book, I traded her a rum sour for this sketch. I am a great believer in the power of rum sours. I learned them from Brad, when he was courting. That was back in Prohibition days, but I have a good memory. Some of you readers, even with good memories, may need to go to history books to learn about Prohibition. Novels of the Roaring Twenties are illustrative. We had English teachers then, too, who tried to teach me not to digress, at least in the middle of a paragraph, but as I said above, I skipped a few things in school.

Here we are, back again in Belize. A Tropical mockingbird, slim and elegant, flies across a net lane and hits, to its bewilderment, this surprising mesh obstacle, getting caught by its clutching feet. No, it's not caught, mockers are smart, it is flopping along, moving faster than I can, I have to watch my own feet if I am not to sprawl over a log. The bird reaches the open end and is gone.

"Smaller, or stupider birds," I tell the pupil I have acquired, now trotting along at my side, "lie quietly until one of us shortly-to-arrive humans comes to disentangle it. Gently. Watch my hands, my index finger, as I remove this sparrow. Bigger birds may flop until they reach one of those tears I haven't yet mended, or the loose end, and are gone just as I reach for them. This is a specialty of doves and hawks, which are big-bodied and strong.

"Indeed I have caught hawks, don't look so disbelieving. Sharpshins and kestrel and merlins; once a Cooper's, though nothing bigger than a Red-shouldered. The same-size mesh, credit it or not, often will hold a hummingbird. If you are trying for hawks you use heavier nets, with a larger mesh. Those won't hold small birds though, and I am a small-bird woman."

Hawks need special techniques, we'll skip these. Louise isn't up to it either.

"Am I confusing you?" I ask my pupil, a newcomer to

banding. "Come along, I'll show you what I'm talking about. We need to check the nets down the dirt road where I left Kleenex guide lines. We check only every half-hour, on cloudy days maybe a little longer, to give birds feeding in the area time to return. We drive them away with our noisy feet and cheery chatter. If nets are in hot sun, like this one—here, give me a hand. Push it up, twist a bit, furl it like a sail—we close them. If it starts to rain, if fog blows in thickly—that happens a lot when you are working shorebirds—you close them. Birds will die in hot sun. In fog or rain their body feathers pull off if they are handled. Birds need their feathers, for insulation, for rain coats. They keep these oiled, in top shape—that's a pun, I didn't mean it, sorry. They use oil from a gland at the base of their spine. Like dogs and cats they can shake water off their pelts.

"No, I don't know where they go in hard rain. Under a leaf, or a log, into a woodpecker hole? If rain can't find them you can't either. Some sit right out in the open, enjoying it. For a while, anyway. Didn't you, when you were a kid? I head for shelter these days, I like to be dry. And I'll bet in the kind of downpours we will get in these rain forests birds do too."

I fall silent, remembering that morning in the Tuxtlas when a *norte* had whirled in over the coastal Mexican mountains, catching us unawares. You couldn't see from one end of a net to the other for the rain. A dozen birds had dashed, panicked, for the safety of big-leaved hardwood trees and had been net-ted. Equally panicked, rain sluicing down my eyeglasses, I had worked at releasing these victims of our scientific greed. I had rolled them inside my sweater, tucked them down inside my shirt, in pockets—anywhere to keep them safe from the force of that rain until I could reach the laboratory and dry them. Woodcreepers, antbirds, tanagers; a special, soaked treasure from our summer woods in the north, a Kentucky warbler. Astonishingly, most of them survived.

"You aren't afraid of snakes?" my tyro asks, a little timidly.

"I'm a fatalist," I answer. "You can't go through life worrying. Something is going to get you sooner or later—a drunken driver, cancer from all those chemicals in our food, on our food, from agricultural sprays. We've banned some of these, but we still export them to other countries, they come back to us on the fruit stands. I suppose I'll feel differently the day I encounter a snake. I never have. The fer-de-lance is the only aggressive one here, that might go for you; one of the rattlers where I worked in Arizona, last spring. The rest get out of your way if you give them a chance. You'll probably see a Green racer, they're common. Another they call Thunder and Lightning, we'll have to ask Dora why.

"In Florida the park rangers suggested I swish a stick in the vegetation ahead of me. You could try that if you wish. I found it a nuisance, only did it for a time or two. By afternoon our feet will have beaten down a path along the nets here, and we'll be able to see anything on them. Remember to look when you step over logs or among rocks, though."

I decide not to tell her about the boa I had picked up by its tail to photograph at Crooked Tree Lagoon, terrifying our guide, but I do tell her about copperheads that bask on the rocks at Carnegie's Powdermill Reserve in Pennsylvania. These did worry me; I kept a sharp watch when I worked there. Once I went on a trail ride in the Appalachians. We camped out at night— my first time ever, a city woman in her forties. I hadn't wanted to sleep in a tent full of women so I asked if I might spread my poncho out in the open. Tom Alexander considered a moment, then consented. He warned me "to thrash around a bit for a while, though" and not to pick a spot close to the old stone walls rattlers den in. What he didn't warn me of were the fishermen who might surprise me when I stripped to bathe in the river. I found that out for myself early the next morning, caught in a pool, a bigger trout than was expected by the fisherman who rounded the bend.

Dora bears a scar where she was struck two years ago by a fer-de-lance. Hideous, I am told, all across her foot where the gangrenous flesh had had to be dug out between the tendons, up her leg. The biggest skin graft ever given in the Miami hospital. They had wanted to amputate, but she wouldn't let them. Fortunately she had been fifteen minutes from serum, she wrote me. "After twenty years in Africa and this country my luck ran out."

I go ahead of my young companion on these paths not yet trodden down, and am watchful. At my age I can afford to be a fatalist. For myself, but not for her. As we hunt Kleenex markers, taking a bird from a net here and there, I keep on talking. An eager listener is a great temptation.

"Like people, given the proper food and habitat birds have reserves that can carry them through the crises of their short lives. Well, not so short if you compare them with us, gram per pound, heart per heartbeat, the use of energy. I don't know how long woodcreepers and Pygmy kingfishers live, but I took a Kentucky warbler in Mexico for John Rappole that he had banded in exactly the same place seven years before. If there is any forest left I'll bet it is still there. Kentuckys don't migrate all that far, though; they breed in the central U.S. Take a robin, everyone knows a robin, they are a dooryard bird. I've banded them from Canada to South Florida. The ones I take on Nantucket in fall have used up their fat flying the Sound and are busy replenishing this on the rosehips and poison ivy berries of the abandoned farm where I work. They weigh between twelve and thirteen grams. That's less than half an ounce. Say two robins to an ounce, thirty-two to a pound, compare that to my regrettably solid one hundred fifty pounds—how many grams do I weigh?"

Who started all this arithmetic? I can darned well tell you who's not going to end it.

"Your heartbeat is seventy-two times a minute. A robin's, well, I don't know a robin's, my figures are in my file up north. Songbirds vary from three hundred fifty to four hundred eighty at rest. A Ruby-throated hummingbird's is five hundred, and can go up to a thousand—you can figure how fast that uses up calories. Different books give you different figures, but you get the idea. A robin lives, say fifteen years—the U.S. Fish & Wildlife's computer has that figure but it is out of date; there must be a new one by now. If you compare this with our biblical three score years and ten, plus a few more that modern medical science has thrown in, we are pretty comparative with robins. Unless I have those figures all wrong, which is quite possible. What I'm saying, I guess, is that birds can be as tough and long-lived as we are, if we don't spray all their foods with poisons. Never *mind* how many years it took me to learn all this, how old I am. You can figure it out from my having been a college lass back in the Roaring Twenties, from my remembering Cal Coolidge's handling of the Big Boston Police Strike, from dancing cheek to cheek—how naughty! how nice!— at Copley Plaza tea dances to Meyer Davis's band. What difference does age make? It's what you have learned, what you know."

And I still don't know where birds go to keep dry in the rain. I've taught this tyro listening to me, well confused but willing, about nets, though. I stand beside her, watching her apply my teaching to freeing a Bentbill. She puts it carefully in one of the small cotton bags we carry birds in, one to a bag. We pick off the ones we had hung on a branch while I taught her and return to see what others have been bringing in to headquarters.

Dave, our official photographer, has set up a studio of sorts under an improvised shelter, a bit apart from the group milling about the record table. In a large box he inserts branches, variously bare or leafy according to the species of bird he also inserts—or small logs, a rock, whatever might be applicable habitat for his subject. He waits patiently. The pose must be as right in stance as his focus, he must constantly adjust shields to control the light. He must also constantly control annoyance as we, in ignorance or impatience, try to hurry him so we can also photograph, out in the open, these birds new to many of us. Someone holds up each one, tipping a colored crown, an open, patterned wing toward the expensive cameras jockeying for position. Some birds are tractable, some flutter, turn their heads away. Some bite.

In a circle on the ground First Day's Class is grouped around bird guides, learning the characteristics to notice as a bird under study (and attendant cameras) is held for comparison. Someone is scanning an erythrina tree, announcing the orioles and tanagers to be seen among its big yellow blossoms. The maid, Maria, arrives with broom and pail to tidy the cottage, assesses the situation, and leaves. Everyone is having a marvelous time. Except possibly, the big red-winged grasshopper that has landed on our worktable and is not at all pleased by the cameras that surround him, the fingers that spread his bright wings. He spreads them himself, when irritated. Dragonflies up north can fly forty miles per hour, I don't know about this one.

Evening

Over coffee, after reviewing the day's birds—there is an argument over a hawk seen only at a distance—we persuade Dora to tell us about the international visitors, the photographers, mammologists, lepidopterists, ornithologists, spelunkers—that's Diane's specialty, she takes people caving—who have fed at these tables, whose names are in her Guest Book, on the fly leaves of her considerable scientific library. Too bad people don't also inscribe their names on the headboards of the beds they sleep in, I say, I'd like to know my predecessors. Or would I? Diane lifts an eyebrow. That big bed is in her house, not Dora's.

In the dim light I accustom my eyes to the shapes of our group, my ear to their voices—this one cheery, enthusiastic, that one sharp, another hesitant. That thin man at the end of our table so far has been entirely silent, but his eyes see everything; he also is studying expressions. His eyes catch mine, smile. I am not usually known for my silence, but in this group I am outdone.

Day 3

I wake to thick fog hanging in the pines, showers of rain that
come and go. I want a clean shirt! I want my yellow suitcase!
The one under my bed holds only towels, books, a slicker I
haven't worn in years, not since that winter in Sunny Arizona
when it rained, or snowed, every day for a month. I don this
latter to go out to the biffy. My companions have gone, leaving neat beds behind them. They must have been mighty quiet.
I had set my inner clock to Oversleep deliberately. And oh,
bliss, I had needed only a sheet to keep me warm, all night.

Going over for breakfast I notice toads along the wet paths.
Vallipses, I am told later; the size of their eyes is dictated by
their parotid glands, I may identify them by the ridges that
run down from their shoulders. What I see, what holds my
attention entirely is not their parotid glands but their lovely
gilt-edged eyelids. Not the finest of human makeup skills could
approximate these.

I notice also an ample supply of poisonwood. A half-inch
seedling of this tree is enough to send me to a medical clinic.
In South Florida it grew all through my woods. Its leaves blistered my cheeks as I ran my net lanes, its seeds sprouted among
the weeds I pulled from my gardens. Must I deal with this

green evil again? It is more virulent than poison ivy, a member of the same genus, *Rhus*. Have I told you about two former expeditions to this country? We lived at a university field station where Dora taught summers, down by the Guatemalan border. This has become a military post, so our studies there went for nothing. In ornithology if you are to end up with anything more than population surveys you need to work in one place over a period of years, to correlate changes in bird life with the changes in vegetation, land use, weather. We had a good time, though, a half-dozen of us there twice, studying birds in the hand we had never seen before. Some species proved unreported, or rare to the country (you will find my name, as reporter, in Peterson and Chalif's *A Field Guide to Mexican Birds*. Misspelled, but what is a misspelling balanced against glory?)

The Mayan families who passed by our nets and work tables, watched us weighing, measuring, and then releasing birds that were perfectly good to eat, thought we were mad. One of the women brought us tortillas wrapped in her scarf for our breakfasts, still warm, delicious. We were not accustomed to tortillas for breakfast, but we learned. In Mexico breakfast tortillas used to come with a bowl of fiery-hot, chopped, green jalapeños. Tears running down our cheeks, we never did learn to accept this substitute for marmalade. With elementary Spanish I arranged with the kitchen to give us their marvelous forest honey. I may be only a pseudo-ornithologist, but I have my uses; I always find my way into kitchens.

Where was I? Poisonwood. I get off the subject. That's all right, we have a whole month ahead of us.

On our second expedition, the day Dora took the others to visit an Indian village her truck wasn't big enough, so Roland Clement and I stayed behind to set up nets. Roland is an eminent naturalist, a writer, a former vice president of the National Audubon Society. Swinging a machete in heat is not what he enjoys, but he was gallant. I carried the saplings a worker had cut for our poles, hoisted on my shoulder. They had been stripped, were slippery with sap. With their mottled bark left on I would have recognized them. Each one had to be set in the ground, which, while Roland hacked manfully at brush, I did; using knees and thighs and arms and cheeks. By mid-afternoon I was blistered and streaming. Fortunately there was a hospital in Punta Gorda—only fifteen miles to drive instead of the full day and overnight to Belize City. Equally fortunately the Mennonite nurses—I think they were Mennonites, they have colonized this country; fine people, good agriculturalists—found a shot of the drug that dries me up, promised to procure more. Cortisone? It begins with a *c*. Whatever, it works miracles. I should wear its name tatooed on my scapulars.

So today, seeing the leaves of these small, shrubby trees glistening along my way to the Main House, I am unhappy. Birds love the berries, particularly big doves. They scatter the seeds everywhere.

I also see those slim-boled palms that are coated with long, vicious spines. Also common in second growth, also in ample supply. When you skid on a hill and grasp for anything to slow your fall, one is always conveniently at hand. The spines will go through sneaker soles, if you step on a fallen bole. They can give you an unpleasant infection. Why don't I stay on Cape Cod? I ask myself crossly. (I haven't yet had my coffee).

Actually I am excited as I look about at the tropical vegetation. Immaculate clouds are piled in a marvelously blue sky. The path opens out at a pond, wind skitters across its surface. An egret, also immaculate, stands in green reeds on the far shore. Fruit trees are fragrant in bloom, small birds flicker in them. A high fence cascades vines where the Main House sits on its stilts. I pass through a gate, skirt a water tank green with moss; a hummingbird whirs past my head. New England winter is far, far away.

Another gate is at the bottom of a wide flight of steps; I expect to restrain the Dobermans. Above, raincoats are heaped on the floor. A buzz of conversation, a fine smell of breakfast comes from the room inside. The Dobermans rise, blocking my passage. They sniff my legs thoroughly, pass judgment, let me enter.

Day 4

First light of dawn, figures moving about the beds. My sheet is damp from the night's humidity. I scratch. Claudia is also scratching, warns that there must be chiggers in the field we used for a shortcut yesterday.

"You talked in your sleep all night," she tells me, "but you sounded so happy I didn't like to wake you."

I apologize.

"Never mind," she smiles. "Marge talked too. Just not at the same time."

Through the outhouse door I admire stars caught in a pine tip. A gibbous moon still glows behind the cottage. My flashlight batteries are low, where are the extras I packed? In that lost suitcase. Dora and Diane shake their heads against a trip to the City. It is too far, the road is rough, the cars in poor shape. On the next necessary run—the end of the week? My pills are in that suitcase too. Well, why should I live forever? I won't drop dead, I often neglect to take them. My doctor is a hypochrondriac. It would be nice to have a different shirt, though. I am wearing one of Diane's. The same one, every day.

On the path we must still use flashlights. The pond gleams

pale under the paled moon. Claudia waxes poetic: "What can ail thee, knight at arms / Alone and palely loitering? / The broome is withered in the sedge / . . ." We can't remember the last line. What does it have to do with the pond anyway? We dredge our memories nonetheless, and come up empty. Halfway through breakfast Claudia shouts triumphantly, "And no birds sing!" We burst into laughter. The rest look at us. Obviously we are crazy. The place is full of singing birds. Claudia is a pleasure to room with, to eat pancakes beside. She is up early but very quiet about it, not using a flashlight. She has been on many bird tours and is well trained. She is always dressed and out before I have finished my slothful yawning and stretching.

As we reach the gate to the compound (I got ahead of myself on those singing birds) and fiddle with its hook, the Dobermans hurl themselves at the fence, reluctantly decide we belong. Probably our jeans, daily dirtier, are beginning to smell? Look on the bright side, I tell myself. With all this running back and forth mine are hanging looser on my hips, in spite of pancakes and all that good food of Diane's I am eating. Diane is a writer, become cook for twelve, to the satisfaction of all. (Well, of us; I very much doubt she enjoys it.) Or are my jeans hanging from the weight of mud on them? I ask myself grumpily. I AM grumpy. I am wearing definitely moist underwear. Along with that shirt. I rinse it and my socks in my shower water at night, hang them on my bedposts to dry, only they don't. My clothes are all in that suitcase somewhere between Boston and Belize. Or Argentina? Anything can get lost in Miami Airport. Except me, after twelve years I knew every inch of it. As long as I was inside; they kept rebuilding the outside.

I wear a borrowed shirt. Diane's—I said that. The insect

repellent I rub on my skin is loaned by generous roommates whose supplies must last them. I need the jeweler's loupe I use to examine birds' skulls, to determine their ages. Pancakes are no substitute for what I am lacking.

I grump my way past three surprisingly early, crisply cottoned ladies. Who are these visitors between me and the coffee pot? I find, too late, that one is the British High Commissioner's wife, with guests. As Elder Stateswoman of our group I am supposed to make an impression. Well, probably I have. Not a good one.

When they leave—I pulled myself together, dug out the diplomatic manners I learned when Brad worked for the Eisenhower Administration, showed them Dave's photography box, our record sheets, the nets; brought them an oriole to admire, its colors glowing in my hand; held a stiff-tailed woodcreeper to their ears so they could marvel at its rapid heartbeat—Diane restores my spirits. She needs to telephone the City. I need to telephone New York.

In the morning heat we drive to Belmopan. In spite of being the capital city it is only a small town, its diminutive wedding cake Mayan capitol set in a small green square bordered by official buildings, a hospital, a post office, a college (? I never found out), bordered in turn by a small market where flapping canvas protects fruit stalls from rain, wares are piled along a few narrow open corridors, smells of coffee and food frying hang in the air. All of this, edged by a gas station and a commercial warehouse, covers only three or four of our city blocks. But there are, surprisingly, two telephone offices. Diane drops me off at the International one, shortly comes running back on foot waving a letter. She and Dora have been commissioned to write a book on wildlife; she is euphoric.

I am not. If that manuscript of mine hasn't been received at my publisher's, it won't matter that I don't have a clean shirt or dry underwear. I will have to go back to the States. Which won't be easy to arrange. I have only an 800, toll-free number for New York, which the two clerks regretfully tell me can't be used on an international line.

We discuss the problem. We try to reach those relatives and friends whose numbers I carry in my head. These aren't many, and they don't answer. Whenever a Belizean comes into the small office my affairs are put On Hold. No sense in getting disagreeable—I have seen too many Ugly Americans go down to defeat in foreign countries. Besides, these two men are trying to help me; or at least the one who hasn't gone out for lunch still is. Diane commiserates, goes off to market, returns. She tried to telephone the airport to see if by a miracle I can obtain a reservation for New York. I should arrive on Fifth Avenue in sneakers and muddy jeans? In a British Army camouflage shirt with a ripped sleeve? Never mind, publishers must take their authors as they come, the editor I talk with has marvelous manners. The National circuits were busy.

At last, as I am close to tears from frustration, the Mayan gods turn my way; I am, after all, a guest in their country. The chief telephone officer, comfortably filled with lunch, in good humor, saunters in, inquires as to my distress, clucks his tongue.

"But if you know the address of your party, Madame, we can of course get the number you wish from the New York Information. No problem."

Madame's and his clerk's jaws drop—no one had thought of such a simple solution out in this jungle clearing. With incredible speed my request goes through, with incredible serendipity that line I may wait on for two hours when I call it from Cape Cod answers. A familiar and welcome voice, magnified by how many relays, booms at me. My manuscript has arrived. Within the hour. Sent Priority Mail, Cape Cod to

New York twelve days ago. But it is in good condition. Go catch a Colobus. (That's a Gerald Durrell animal and book title. Probably the nearest my urban editor knows to a bird name.)

The Belizean official beams, clasps my hand across the counter.

"You see, Madame? You are in the capital of this country, in Belmopan. We run things well." He presents a bill for $7.50 U.S.—less than it would have cost me to talk with New York at home!

When your number is reached from this International Office, a room the size of a small kitchen, you are directed to a private booth, fan-cooled, with a Rest Room adjacent in case you have become nervous. After failing to reach four different cities in the U.S. I could have used a shower . . .

Now *I* am euphoric. "Where," I ask Diane, fitting into her little car, "is the liquor store?"

Rum is the cheapest intoxicant in this country. We drink it before dinner, to relax the physical stress of our days. With twelve of us a bottle doesn't last long. I need a bottle.

Diane then reports my suitcase is safely at the airport and she must go into the City on Saturday, only three days away; she can fetch it then.

I change my order to "A *case* of rum! And where is that manuscript you want me to type for you?" To ensure the arrival of that suitcase I will do anything *"Amor con amor se paga."*

In celebratory mood we decide to eat lunch in one of the two restaurants, under a fan. In the Chinese one, Diane suggests, the food is better, if the décor is plain. Its room proves royal blue in paint. Christmas decorations sparkle over the tables, Coke cases are piled in geometric patterns. Except for the fact that the pinups of calendar girls picture old-fashioned, decorous dresses it could be any backwoods restaurant in America. The beer is cold, the juke box blessedly not in use. We stuff on hot lobster salad full of frozen U.S. vegetables, too much to finish. Never mind the expense, this is a celebration. We toast the U.S. Post Office, my editor, my yellow suitcase in tea that has a lump of ice in it, which must double its price. The temperature outside is 95°F., with corresponding humidity. We talk up a storm, we are in no hurry.

Emerging at last, we find we are locked out of the Nova. Diane's survival techniques (she teaches Survival to the British Army; I'll tell you about that in a minute) does not extend to this emergency. But this is our day of good fortune. A Good Samaritan saunters up. With practiced dexterity (practiced how? Where? We don't ask him) he runs a wire through the window slit, unhooks our key, manages not to drop it on the floor, presents it to Diane with a flourish. We return to the restaurant to buy him a beer and again enjoy the whirring fans.

I have to wonder about our cook, Diane. She is a slim, handsome woman with a great coil of dark hair that I should think would handicap her activities of caving, rock climbing, mountaineering. She is a crack shot, has been a member of a prestigious club in Britain. She is an informal Survival Instructor, consultant here in Belize to the British Army's SAS Corps, on which our Green Berets are modeled. It must be a trick to teach men of this caliber, and have them accept her! She teaches survival to lesser groups, too, knowing the mountains. She says some in the west are so rugged they have not yet been adequately explored. She supplements her income by taking tourists camping if she feels they can deal with the rigors.

She is a writer—the Smithsonian is dealing with her and Dora, on wildlife in Central America. She has been married, twice, colorfully. Her first husband lives nearby, he comes over to repair our equipment. Their child, a nice ten-year-old lad, was with us for dinner last night. Her second husband, older, rich, turned out to have not one but two other wives and shortly disappeared.

She moves with extraordinary grace, a long skirt swirling about her ankles. She is an indomitable talker, standing in the door of her kitchen, eyes flashing, spoon waving. I am fascinated by her stories, the play of her mind. If I sit to listen she goes off, so I stand until my legs ache. She has never cooked for a group before, but she is momentarily broke, momentarily free. It is a different form, she laughs, of survival. I am amazed by her frankness. Perhaps people whose lives burst with activity haven't time to hide, to conceal. I don't know whether she likes me or whether she talks equally frankly—and equally long—to the others, but then, I am around more than they are. I certainly like her. She has let me into the kitchen—after a bit of training—which is definitely a privilege.

She has given me a whodunit she hopes to have published about a female assassin, also thirty-four, who, like herself, relaxes by rock climbing. It is a violent book, but Diane has led a violent life on several continents. When she takes that long glossy hair down I watch covertly to see if a knife or a dagger slides out of it. Not yet. . . . I wonder at her easy knowledge of the techniques and psychology and associates of the assassin profession, and wonder too if the Smithsonian suspected these talents when they suggested a contract?

Her story is fast-paced, gripping. I put it down last evening only because the lights of our Common Room were doused. Today I am back into it, editorial pencil in hand, hair crawling on the back of my neck. I have lived a protected life, my only scars are on my legs and ego.

Day 5. Morning

I am running the ranch. Everyone else left, early and eager, for a distant banding area. After giving me a lesson in stove lighting Diane has gone to the City to shop, to pick up my suitcase at the airport and that handsome new man, a Colonel. There is no bed for him, but somehow this will be worked out. Somehow in this country everything gets worked out. It would give my New England sense of order ulcers to live here.

I have offered to make bread, to vary the expensive product purchased from our neighbor, who has only one version, tasty but too crumbly for sandwiches. Bread on our table disappears as fast as it can be sliced. I enjoy making bread. Also it would be nice to sort out my few possessions in daylight. I have some typing to do, a book I'd like to read, but mostly I am Guardian of the Ranch, like the Dobermans stretched at my feet.

On her hands and knees Maria scrubs the verandah, singing a little as she works. She would rather scrub than sweep, she says. I love being here alone with Maria and the dogs. Contented, peaceful. It isn't what I came to these tropics for; my purpose was Useful Work. But this relaxation is balm to my spirit, working out the tangles my psyche has snarled in as I see myself growing old. I am unwilling to accept the restrictions of my years.

Below the railing, orioles talk to each other in the caliandra bush, like a family berry picking in a field. I follow their progress by the movement of the leaves, glimpses of a tail, a bright eye, a patch of orange. They feed inside the foliage. On the outside a hummingbird buzzes the pink powderpuff flowers, its wings a shimmering blur. If I inadvertently move, if Maria comes through the kitchen door all the birds are gone (although the dogs are accepted). They belong in a world unrelated to ours, "gifted with extensions of the senses we have lost or never attained, living by voices we shall never hear. They are not our brethren, they are not underlings, they are other nations, caught with ourselves in the net of life and time."

Henry Beston wrote those lines, when he was living in Outermost House on a Cape Cod beach I have tramped many summers watching, as he must have, young Least terns and Piping plovers scamper on his sands. His little house is gone now, washed away by the great winter storm of February 1978; the dunes that sheltered him are gone. Now where they were—it's hard to be sure, the landmarks are gone too—is an uneven grass and pebbled expanse where terns settle when they come north from South America to nest. Now it is harder for me to walk in that heavy sand than it was ten years ago to count the birds, to hope that skunks and fox and other nocturnal prowlers don't find them. Now the bay on the other side of Beston's beach where Champlain, long before both of us, anchored his fleet is a wide marsh, its grasses bending to the wind, verdant in summer, golden in fall. The tides creep, shining among grass stems. Life is change.

Afternoon

I am still lazing on the verandah, waiting for visitors I am to guide to our forest nets. I am reading an article by an intellectual woman I admire, about dying. It is not death that bothers her as much as the process, the mental and physical losses that come with age. She is not much younger than I, maybe I should start worrying too? Because I also am encountering those small humiliations she resents. I am not as eager as I used to be to run around with our work crew, slipping and sliding in mud. The other day one of them actually said, "Let me go down there, Jonnie, that bank is too steep."

Hah! Afraid she might have to boost, or haul my weight back up? I showed her. But she was right, it was steep, I had to do it on my knees.

In her article my writer discusses deterioration over tea, with friends. They are thinkers also, who like to discuss life's problems, work out ways to handle them. My trouble is that any friends with whom I might discuss are younger; they aren't about to discuss dying, they are too busy talking about what they are going to do next year. They also talk about what *I* am going to be doing with them next year. That's pretty nice.

One of the difficulties of living alone is that no one—well, yes, my plumber, eying my furnace, kicking rust flakes off my water tank; my neighbor, worrying about a pine that will fall across his driveway in some winter storm—wants to discuss Age with me, and what I should do about it. I don't care to discuss Age either, no matter how it nibbles at my carcass. You'd think my doctor might, handing me another bottle of pills, but all he does is pat my shoulder. No talker he, I am left on my own. If I start worrying about the mess my business files are in, the antique table I should refinish for a grandchild, I put Mozart or some country yodeler on my record player, look at figure skating on TV, plant more daffodils in my garden. Not constructive, but there is no one to chide me. One of the pleasures of living alone.

What mostly worries the writer of this article is immortality. She craves it. She wants her books and teaching to carry her philosophies into the future. Laudable but impractical; we part company here. I see an individual's life as a book. Full—or empty—of interest, of successes and failures, of love, of adventure. Possibly an inspiration to others, as she desires, but probably not too much. What matters deep down, what carries us through our days, however selfish, is what life gives *us* in the way of richness and satisfaction. I don't say happiness; that is a will of the wisp. Satisfaction is what you build on. We reach out and touch other people but when we are gone our book is closed, it goes on a shelf. We live only in memories until the people who remember us are also gone.

Memories fade, people have other concerns. Our furniture is discarded. My successor will turn my garden into a parking place, the trees I've planted will be cut down. The herbs by the back door, my blue curtains blowing in the sea breeze . . . they will go.

So we had better pick the flowers in our garden to take to a friend; share our happinesses while we are here.

"But you have children," this woman might say. "You live on through them. My only immortality is in my books."

I am cynical. I shudder to think of what my grandparents would say of their descendants if they should put their heads into one of our modern homes, how appalled they might be by—well, at least the surface trappings of—their immortality.

And did you ever ask a class of youngsters to write down the first names of their grandparents? How many could? Can you? Those lives are dusty books, packed away. Those lives are headstones tipped by frost, where deer run at night.

Who could I talk with about this article, loan it to in our group? Henry is the nearest to my age, I'll go talk to Henry. He went up the path a while ago with his camera, determined to find a miniature passion flower. He and I saw one, marked the place, when we came back it had disappeared. I found another later on the path to the Main House (as in the childhood story, the bluebird of happiness is in your own back yard), but Henry wasn't with me. He'll be more interested in the death of passion flowers (which evidently bloom only in the morning) than in his own. A proper attitude.

Day 6

The nets have been moved from scrub to pine savanna, within walking distance. There is a small stream beyond, I haven't seen it. It is productive, the others get there first. So why not let them? I am on call for emergencies, only we don't have any. And if we did who am I to step in ahead of our professionals, as joyful as kids in this country new to them?

But as I live the nearest, am not one who needs coffee to open my eyes, I skin out early this morning, while the chachalacas are still calling; soaking my sneakers in the tall grass and shallow puddles, slipping on mossy corduroy logs. In heavy fog I open the nets, shake the water from them, tighten guy lines. An acorn woodpecker with a red, white, and black clown face—I had these in Arizona too—supervises me, then flies to a wind-bent pine to dispute territory with a rival. I look down more than up, needing to watch my steps. Clumps of grass are ornamented with filmy white baskets surprisingly tough to the touch. The home of some spider, I forget its name: fuzzed and thickened by dew they will become less visible when the sun has dried their silken threads.

Colorless in the fog a hawk flies over the empty fields. I turn off in the hope of seeing it more closely but evidently it finds the fields empty too, it flies away. We are both wanting breakfast.

I spend much of the day cross-legged on the ground beside Dave. He perches on his big metal carrying case, focused on that glass-fronted box he must assemble and disassemble each day, each rainstorm. Each bird new to our list goes into this through a sleeve—that's my job—acquaints itself with its cage, comes finally to rest on a branch for its portrait. Only as birds have minds of their own, it is as apt to perch backward as forward, to dig itself into a leafy corner, to hold its head at the wrong tilt. Dave is frustrated; I enjoy what could be an interesting series of behavior studies. Each species has its own method of settling in, of expressing resentment; they aren't alarmed, just uncooperative. Dave is enormously patient. He changes perches, cuts different branches, coaxes, swears. At the perfect instant his subject will move a wing, droop a leg out of position. He talks to them as he might to a child bewildered by a new circumstance. He cares. His photographs are carried in national magazines.

Behind us the working crew comes and goes, taking birds out of the brightly colored bags they hang on trees: like flowers, waiting. They discuss depths of bills and eyelines, signs of mature or juvenile feathering, the possibility of finding a rare species down by that stream I finally get to (finding nothing at all in the nets). Technical talk I enjoy.

Still Day 6, it's been a long day.
It is night now, though.

If it is foggy tomorrow morning when alarm clocks give out their digital beeping—one in our room, one a minute later from the lower floor, I can turn over and sleep another hour, only subconsciously aware of rustlings and quiet footsteps. If it is clear I have offered to act as secretary on a transect run.

I haven't told you about transects? We do them every other day, first thing in the morning. They are a chore, so far I have managed to miss them. They are technical, if you want to miss them too I won't be offended. But that's what I'll be doing early tomorrow, with Chan. Perhaps a dozen times over the years I have been fortunate to work with Chan—Chandler S. Robbins, one-third author of *The Birds of North America,* in my opinion far and away the best identification guide yet published, now in revision. He has a God-given gift—but first let me describe a transect. As I said, they are technical. You can skip, we can't.

A transect is a method of estimating bird populations. A series of equidistant checkpoints (10 in this case) is marked out, each point with an imaginary 30-meter (in this case) circle. Each circle is separated by 100 meters so there is no overlap, so that birds active in one will presumably not be recorded in the next. The observer stands at the checkpoint with its orange marker and dictates to a secretary (in this case me) the species he sees or hears, in what vegetation, how high, engaged in what activity—feeding, resting, flying, preening, defending. The observer himself must see and hear the bird, although his elbow may be plucked, for attention. (I suspect this is against the rules, but not mine.) In exactly five minutes the talliers move to the next numbered orange ribbon on its bush and repeat. There is no conversation. I have no responsibility but attentiveness and legible handwriting.

There, that wasn't too bad, was it? It's the "no conversation," of course, that makes it dull to me.

Day 7

The day proves overcast, neither one nor the other. I didn't wash my clothes last night so they are dry, great! I hurry along the trail, over the bridges, past the pond, its surface motionless and pale, to the Main House for coffee, an orange, and a hard-boiled egg left over from yesterday's lunch. I have just begun to eat when Chan finishes, tucks his jeans into his boots and hands me the clipboard that is my badge of office. My coffee is too hot. I can't choke down a whole egg at once. Regretfully I abandon them, pocket the orange, and follow my leader's brisk, long-legged strides. Imperceptibly—probably he hears me puffing—he slackens them.

Chan has, I started to say, the God-given gift of perfect pitch. He can hear and recognize sounds most other people can't, is sensitive to the slightest subtle difference in each separate chip, chuck, chirr, whippety-whee of hundreds of bird species. He can say to our group, perfectly calmly as we pause along a road to check out a Meadow lark, "Do you notice it has eighty percent of the notes of an Eastern, and only twenty percent of the Western song?" No, naturally the rest of us haven't.

He has also a God-given sweetness that keeps him from ever

putting an amateur down. Years ago when I was a beginner
he encouraged and motivated me, taught me—no, steered me
into learning for myself. If he has an ego it is not visible to
me. He is the pleasantest and most rewarding of companions.
I dislike transects, but I will go with him anytime. I should
think the others would fight to replace me.

How many years ago was it we went out hunting chuck-
will's-widows one evening in Maryland? We discuss this as we
head for the first orange ribbon. It was after I had moved to
Florida. I had been flattered into giving a program—my first
to a real ornithological meeting—about my work in Everglades National Park. I didn't, and still don't, know enough
to address serious birders, but I must have been successful, for
I have been giving programs ever since. (Please remember the
difficulty program chairmen have lining up enough speakers,
one a month, preferably noncontroversial.) I have no memory
at all of the meeting, but I could recount every detail of walking down that country lane in the dusk with Chan, hunting
chucks.

He dictates what I am to write in which column on my pad.

"Look out for this vine," he warns, holding up a branch as
I pass it. "The leaves will slice your face like a razor. Do you
hear that warbler?"

I beam at him. After a struggle with my vanity I have bought
a hearing aid. I have a dozen friends I wish would too. We
wear glasses, special shoes, braces, take medication, why should
we be humiliated to admit deafness? I am hearing high notes
of warblers I haven't heard in years, am learning again to differentiate their calls. I also can hear the light voices of children, and even what some of those people say whose voice is
more breath than resonance, who talk inside their mouths,
who block their voices with fingers or a book, turn their backs

and still expect you to know what they are saying! I still miss a lot, but you can miss, I have decided, and often be little the worse for it. People talk too much anyway. Including me. This isn't to say I am fond of this little pink artifical aid to keep senior citizens functioning. I lose it, I misplace it. I've had to insure it; I forget and wear it swimming, in salt water. At parties it is difficult to filter out what my partner is saying from the background buzz and clatter. The crunch of our boots as we walk through the wet grass this morning is surprisingly painful, as is the rattle of my notebook paper. Never mind—I can hear Chan's warbler.

By the time we have finished our stint we are properly hungry. On our way home I volunteer for the next stint. I am comfortable working with men, waiting on them, making myself a part of the interesting work they do. Men know best, my father taught me. I've learned since that they don't always, but I don't tell them unless it becomes really necessary. Even then there are ways; you can just disappear. I don't like arguments. My father was a proper Victorian. My granddaughters would never take him seriously. I don't myself, now.

Diane is waiting for us, pancake spoon at the ready. The others have eaten and gone. I can go or stay as I want, she says, with a meaningful glance at her ancient typewriter. She has written a whodunit—I told you. She wants to write a series around her lady assassin; these are icing on the cake of her scientific papers. I am editing this one for her. I have told you that, too, and that I am always getting into tasks I'm not suited for. But I so enjoyed my publisher's editing of my manuscript, admired his diplomatic handling of me, of the ways in which he led me to shift and clarify my pages, that I want to try my hand at this. The diplomacy worries me—it is easier for a man to criticize a woman than another female. It will be a challenge.

I opt to stay. Diane is pleased. She must go down the highway later on errands. If her little green car balks on the road she needs someone with her to sit in it while she hitches a ride for help. If there is to be any car—any tires, spark plugs, gasoline in it when she returns.

In my usual evening corner by the window I am ostensibly scribbling notes on our day's activities, but my mind is far away. Something—my reflection in the window, the smells preparatory to a meal, the stir of busyness about me—has triggered a memory. I am flying across the United States. It is a long trip from the Pacific rollers crashing on the rocks of Point Lobos, seal heads bobbing just beyond the waves, to the dunes of my gray Atlantic where fishing fleets follow each other irregularly over the bars at this hour. My inertia has been broken by a crying baby, the stewardess's attentions, the rising decibels of women wearing conference labels on their flowered bosoms. Clearly they are having one martini too many to ease the long flight.

I have been considering, on that plane, how I drift about the world in a sort of cocoon of widowhood. Should I keep in aimless motion? Or should I try to break out of my cocoon? Some hour when the timing, the amount of sunlight (inner or outer) becomes just right, will I metamorphose? If so, into what? The hours drag, I am trying to occupy my mind, bored with my book and the aircraft magazines. I try to decide whether my cocoon is corporeal, woven from threads of my emotional state and my loneliness, or is it cultural?

These past few years I have lived not only in differing physical habitats but in an equal number of cultures. After my years of travel on Commerce Department missions as "wife accompanying husband," then by myself with naturalist groups, habitats pose few problems of adjustment for me. I have enjoyed the contrasts of wilderness or city, of hot water or only cold, or of none at all; of a bed in decorator luxury or a mattress on a grandchild's rug, a couch versus a tent; the brisk seawinds of Maine or California; the torrid humidity and downpours of the tropics.

I find more difficult the subtle cultural shifts as I move among the homes of relatives and friends. When there were two of us we carried our culture with us, presented a unified front, could retreat into our own ingrained attitudes and customs with a shared smile across a room, or by closing the door of our personal quarters. Now, alone, I try to fit myself into the patterns of the homes I visit. I feel I must submerge Myself, not try to rock the various boats in which my children, siblings, hosts, or hostesses plough the seas of their lives. I become a stuffed figure, an image. It is a game, of sorts, which I can play successfully only for a few days. Then, unless I move on, my veneer cracks, Myself demands to emerge, disgraces me.

My naturalist friends, who have not yet built up an image of me, know this game also. We may jockey a bit to see who throws the dice but sooner or later we discard our pretenses, kick off our social shoes, and enjoy ourselves. Why can't families adjust as easily? Why do we—or is it just me?—feel a need for pretense? It is dishonest, a hiding, a cheating. We like people for their warts and shadows, the blaze and deviant lines of their curves and opinions, not for their images.

The stewardess had come down the aisle of that plane, wishing to pull my window curtain so the flickering scenes of secondhand living on a movie screen might be more visible, but I wouldn't let her. I was looking out at the real world, its geology, history, and land uses spread below us in sunset light—at the patterns of wrinkled deserts, the gleam of nourishing rivers, the destructive, productive smokestacks belching as we slid down to pause by great cities.

"Sorry," I told her. "I like my living firsthand."

She had shrugged, displeased. She was accustomed to a world lived in boxes—in a plane, a hotel room, an apartment near an airport where planes roar ceaselessly overhead; an impermanent world.

Staring out my window as our huge ship hurtled through the winds, that baby crying, the shrilling of those beflowered women about me, I had wrestled with the uncertain, shy woman Brad's death had made of me, trying to find a center on which I could balance. It is easier to observe and be mannerly, to draw curtains, to look at the lives of others than it is to participate. It isn't easy, alone, to stand out in the round, hair tousled, stockings twisted, to be seen and liked—or disliked—for what you are. But if I was frightened as a single person I had to embrace courage. I had to learn. Life is learning, no matter how painful. Every day, for everyone. Look about you in that plane, I bade myself as the lights came on, at the other travelers. They are all learning—even if only their limit on martinis.

And finally, somewhere over Pennsylvania, as the stewardesses again rattled down the aisle with their carts, I accepted myself as entitled to a space on the huge hurtling airship of Earth, also traveling through the winds of the Unknown. My face reflected back to me from a window. Its lines wavered with our motion through the air currents, as I also surely would in the motions of life's currents. But this was me, Myself, a woman with whom I could learn to live at ease, of whom I need not be ashamed.

I look now about our dim room in Belize for a hand to pull me back from this excursion into my past. The stewardess on that plane had thought I needed a drink. The friendly man Diane brought up with my suitcase yesterday thinks I need a drink, too. He inspects my glass, refreshes it without asking, sits down beside me. He is used to dealing with people, you don't hide or cheat with him. I let him take the pencil from my hand. A window reflects us. Myself there, met again; still wavering, but now I am not running for shelter. On that long air journey I had found my balance, a center from which I can operate. Lifting my glass, I smile at my companion over its rim—a toast that is to myself as well as to a new friend.

Day 8

At home when I must be off and away early to help young grad students working on beach birds or tree swallows, students who need my official permit to band gulls or black-crowned night herons, I roll out of bed, swallow breakfast, and am gone. The roads are edged with the clear yellows of broome or buttercups and dandelion types, depending on the season; flowers—weeds—that hitched their way from Europe in the hay and grain of colonial days. Fog will mist the trees and my windshield. There is fog here today too, hanging in the vines, laying a blanket on the surface of the pond, and obviously I am homesick! In the Common Room people clutter around the coffee table—cheerful chatter from the morning types, dull silence from those who will bloom and chatter before dinner when we morning people have subsided. Gradually they disappear—for transect duty, on a hike to the distant river, to their cottages. Sun breaks through, the day falls into shape. Finally only two of us are left.

Along with my suitcase the other day Diane brought an additional member to us. He is a retired Colonel, stocky, with a bristly head of white hair. A fine twinkle in his eye provokes an answering, bubbling twinkle inside me. He has authority, kept in reserve; he is going to be a useful addition. Not as keen a birder as the women who invited him, who have been looking forward to his arrival, who enjoy correcting him when he mixes up his bird names (as I also do). He is comfortable to sit beside, no need to talk. So, bringing in the last platter of pancakes from the kitchen, I do. I study him to see if he is going to be one of my charmers. I am vulnerable to charmers. They excite me, add a joyous dimension to living, we are hilarious together. Sooner or later they will prove feckless, or find me too staid, we will spin off on separate ways. No regrets.

This man has too much integrity, I decide, to be a charmer. Besides, the other women have set their caps for him, I'm not competitive. I'm not hunting, never was. Men seem to recognize this and admit me into friendship as an equal (if men and women are ever equals). They protect me; I *love* to be protected. The Colonel and I clear the tables together. He swabs them down, I set books and chairs in order, we take our coffee mugs out into the sun on the verandah, each with a dog by our feet.

"You are the silent one around here, Miss Jonnie," he says. "Who are you?"

"Just a retired housewife," I answer him cheerily, laughing at the idea of my being silent. I am always talking. Well, maybe not here, I haven't had much chance. "Is it my personal or my professional history you are asking for?" Light striking his dark glasses reflects, distorts me.

Who am I? How I wish I knew! I am not even she who came through this door an hour ago. Although I wear the same jeans, a teeshirt emblazoned with a tern, some of my cells, visible to a scientist's lens, have divided; new ones have taken their places, subdivided.

Doubtless there are equal cellular changes in the dirt on my jeans, which need laundering. They will dry in this morning's bright sun. I slosh them later in minimum water, in a tub under the house. The Colonel has also gone about his business after fetching me his laundry; I will do that too, I told him. Why not, if I am just a housewife? I think on Change.

I can tell you what I've done, more or less. Where I've been—the countries, the states, the homes, some of the hotels. Restless at night, I even try to list the beds I've slept in. It's more effective than counting sheep. It would certainly take longer, except that I fall asleep in bemused memories of Japanese brick pillows, pillows of feathers, straw, no pillows at all. But who the woman is, or was, who slept on them. . . . I hunt for her sometimes these nights, too, although this is not as restful. We all change, year to year, month to month, hour to hour. But each of us must have some central core that controls us, so that when we meet ourselves coming and going we face what it is we can or cannot do. It is this core that others must recognize as *us,* however much we blind ourselves to it, however much we try to overlay it.

I *am* just a retired housewife. I have no professional training, I tell those book and bird and garden clubs, students, senior citizen groups, businesswomen, the varied organizations I talk to. I am trying to persuade them—they ask for it—that there is a wide, wonderful world out there that needs them, that needs a far better understanding of conservation, of the interrelatedness of everything on our planet, a tolerance of creatures other than smug *Homo sapiens,* a stewardship of the oceans and deserts and forests and suburban yards where they live. I urge them to be activists, in any field. There is every kind of work that needs doing, I tell them, far more urgent than making cookies and casseroles for a luncheon such as they are about to serve me. I eye the men as firmly as the women.

They want to know what I do, how I got into it, how they might get into it. So while it goes against my grain I make my talk personal, I am trying to stir them into action.

I didn't care what I did after Brad died. I lucked into amateur ornithology, but it could have been a half-dozen other fields. Archaeology: I was in Guatemala and the University of Pennsylvania crew, excavating the Mayan temples at Tikal, suggested I join them. But I might have landed in the botany of rain forests, teaching at youth camps—anything as long as it was outdoors and exhausting, as long as it was in another world from the one I had been cut off from. I tell them how I raised a baby fawn and was a waterskiing shill (in my fifties!) at an Adirondack lodge; how I accompanied a man to Peru as his secretary (and guardian from the ladies; he was an attractive fellow). I had a little Spanish; I helped with a university class in Ecuador for the same reason. I went through every door that opened to me, no matter how often I tripped on the sills. I moved to Florida at the suggestion of a biologist I had known ten days and worked there, winters, for twelve years. When I didn't know a tern from a seagull I brashly ran a survey up the Atlantic coast on Least terns for the U. S. Fish & Wildlife Service, continued it for five years, learning as I went, became the grandmother of Least tern protection. I worked at the Cornell Laboratory of Ornithology and the Manomet Bird Observatory, ending up on their Boards because I knew them from the bottom up, instead of from the top down, as the banking and fund-raising members did. This led me to the National Audubon Board, to The Nature Conservancy. I fall asleep at Board Meetings and during fund-raising discussions, but sometimes I can manage to work my way, through back doors, to where I belong.

I am careful, when I give these programs, to wear a frilly, feminine blouse, lipstick, and have my cropped hair neat. I refer casually to my Vassar and Washington backgrounds. It seems a bit dishonest. I give glimpses—only colorful ones, that is dishonest too—of work I've done in glamorous foreign lands. Which aren't glamorous at all when you are working in them, at least not by travel agent standards. The rewards, I assure them, are solid. I have no more training than they have, I'm just restless—widow restless. And willing to take a risk, to say YES to whatever comes along.

I get my reward for these talks when someone seeks me out, writes later to say she—sometimes he—took my advice, it changed her life, she wants to thank me. Saying YES changed my life too, I'm only sharing.

"Why haven't your remarried?" I get that question often.

"I can't," is my answer. "My name is carved on a granite headstone on a Vermont hillside. How can I decently add a hyphen and another name?"

I used to drive to Vermont every year to stand by the generations quiet beneath their stones. It destroyed me, and what good did it do them? If need comes, when I need help, I have only to close my eyes to be there in spirit, stars clear above us on a windy night, spring sunlight paler than memory. The wind soughs through the spruces in summer, deer step delicately in winter. Actually I don't want to lie under a granite marker, even by Brad. I want my ashes buried where they will nourish wildflowers and ferns along the Battenkill. Brad always gave me anything I wanted, but I have conventional children, they won't want to scatter me by a river. It doesn't matter. I won't be there.

My new friend the Colonel didn't get this spiel, although he pinned me down in the kitchen later. I was kneading dough on a mahogany table. How many cooks do you know who can roll their cinnamon bread on solid mahogany? The Colonel was interested in studies I have done on three remote Arizona ranches for The Nature Conservancy.

"Wait a few months," I told him. "It's all in a book just going to press. You are looking at a fugitive from a copy editor. How many may I send you?"

He settles for a Mayan quotation I have pinned above this beautiful table. It is an instruction to a surviving tribe of the Omec-Maya civilization.

> The roots of all living things are tied together. When a mighty tree is felled, a star falls from the sky: before you cut down a mahogany tree you should ask permission of the keeper of the forest, and you should ask permission of the keeper of the star.*

*Victor Perera and Robert D. Bruce, *The Landon Mayas of the Mexican Rain Forest* (Boston: Little, Brown, 1983).

Day 9

This morning I found a scorpion, dead in my toilet kit. I haven't been shaking out my sneakers the way I was taught to in Arizona; maybe I just should. (If I tell you that scorpions are related to spiders, ticks, and mites, forming the class Arachnida, I will have to do the same for jaguars and mice and hummingbirds, and for *Homo sapiens,* so I won't.)

A scorpion bite on a toe may or may not be painful, but the swelling means you don't wear shoes for a while. I learned to be watchful in my small farm cottage in South Florida, although the baby snake I found curled in my underwear drawer one cold morning startled me more. In winter there I often saw a snake coiled in the warmth under my hot-water tank. An Indigo, a big one, one evening eased itself into the old dynamite box I was raising mice in, in my kitchen. I used mice to bait hawk traps—Balchatri traps. (See? That explanation I went into on Balchatris back there on my basement floor is turning out to be useful.)

Indigos are harmless, handsome, and in Florida protected by law. They came in different sizes about my property. Small boys always wanted to take one home for a pet, which would produce a Fisk Lecture. You leave creatures where you find them, I made clear. Where their food supply is, so also is their home and family. Creatures have families just like you, and larders. The lads understood this latter need, although my firmness had more influence. The only Indigo that bothered me was an old one thick as my arm that learned about my hanging birds in those bags I carried birds in to my workshop. The Indigo took up residence on my top shelf, sneaking inside when I was out collecting. I didn't mind if it tried for an occasional red-winged blackbird—it's hard to swallow a mesh bag—but I was wrathy the day a brilliant blue Indigo bunting slipped from my fingers, flew to the shelf, and the Indigo seized him. Practically a cousin, I pointed out, myself seizing, taking my reptile boarder by the base of its neck and heaving it out the door. Go look for scorpions, I admonished it.

That first year we banded with Dora at the Columbia Forest Station a furry spider nearly the size of my palm lived in the bathroom of the cottage Dora and I shared. George, Dora had named him: when you live with someone he needs a name. His territory was the shower curtain and the toilet. The top of the latter had a big crack into which George would scramble if he heard us coming. I took care he always heard me; I wanted to know exactly where he was: better inside that tank than under the seat. . . . He snacked on the abundant small, pale insects—wood roaches? Dora wasn't sure—that ran over and under our pillows at night. Harmless but ticklish. The tarantulas ate these too. Tarantulas aren't fearsome monsters, though it does give you a start to find one inside your bra as Dora did one morning, dressing. Or beside your chair (and feet) in the dining room. We appointed Roland Clement, the naturalist who let me carry those poisonwood poles, our White Knight and Tarantula Remover. At an anguished wail, or merely a plaintive summons from the more experienced, he would pop a glass over, slide a sheet of paper under our baneful visitor, and take it outside. Whence, of course it would return, but not always immediately. The creatures gathered—well, probably only two really—under our table evenings and interfered with his dinner. A naturalist learns to live with wildlife (given time and no choice). I worried more about the small green snake, knitting-needle slender, that lived in a vine on our porch and swung out at me when I passed, gaping its red mouth in fearsome fashion. I have a photograph of it that I use in lectures; you can practically hear it hiss. "Use everything" is my motto. I never did learn to live happily with the pauraque whose bedtime station was the windowsill by my bed. He had a gaping mouth too, it hollered on and on and on and on into the otherwise silent nights. I tried to accept his calls as an expression of love, a moonlight serenade (moon or not), as there seemed no way to dislodge his attentions. I did tape his calls—if you can't lick 'em, join 'em. Use everything. . . . His eyes shone ruby red in the beam of my flashlight.

George. I gave a program once in Lake Wales, Florida, spending the night with new friends. The minuscule guest bathroom was not big enough, I felt, for me and a very large "housekeeping spider" similar to Dora's, so I took a water glass and gave it the Clement treatment, laughing about my success at dinner to my hosts. They were indignant.

"George? You put George OUTSIDE?" I was in disgrace. Not only was he a household pet but a servant, a guardian with an excellent appetite for less desirable visitors. He was back the next morning, though, to supervise my shower.

In an Arizona desert home I often visit I am like as not to find a cache of sunflower seeds under my pillow at night, or in my sneakers, mornings. A note from my hostess warns guests of this, but what can you do, she apologizes, when the desert, which to the uninitiated looks so empty, teems with life? Lives? Particularly mice? Actually I have never met her bedroom mouse, but each evening a family of javelina (collared peccary), big, ugly, snouted beasts, come to her kitchen door for raw potatoes. A ringtailed cat (or several?) tightropes along a wire to hummingbird feeders until each one is licked empty. From their roof a coatimundi will lean, pulling up the jars of sugar syrup also set out for hummers. His tilted, delicate nose is sensitive as a surgeon's fingers. Skunks, gray fox, raccoons drink sugar water too. The skunks, handsome in their black and white pelts, each one individually marked, seem to be at the bottom of the pecking order. This surprises me; I would judge a skunk's arsenal to be the most effective. After an Evening Exhibit of Wildlife on the Desert I check the catches on my bedroom screens carefully, preferring my critters outside.

Where did this start? With that scorpion under my toothpaste tube. How far the mind ranges . . .

I meditate as to whether I should show this scorpion to my roommates, decide against. It is small, and dead. Dottie, a city woman dismayed by our lack of hot water, is not yet comfortable with the outhouse; I shouldn't add to her worries. We haven't yet warned her about the army ants, hoping they will not return. For our sakes also.

WHAT? I HAVEN'T TOLD YOU ABOUT THE DAY THE ARMY ANTS MARCHED THROUGH THE OUT-HOUSE? It's better forgotten. I run on about my past life page after page; why don't I tell you about what really matters?

To reach the ladies' biffy you go around our house, through a gate in the barbed wire fence we have fastened open, what with all the traffic; trip over roots and rocks. Something of a chore in the night—I always run into barbed wire. Dottie had never used a biffy and is, we judge, appalled by it: mostly by its lack of privacy, for while its back is turned politely to passersby, there is no door, and the cracks are sizable; she has been surprised a few times. City folk are used to doors and locks, the basic functions of life tucked out of sight. As I say, we have not told her about the army ants. Maybe they won't return.

We have told her, quite sharply since our own comfort is concerned, that she may not do a daily laundry in the wash-basin. She doesn't understand that when the watertank beside the house is empty it may be months before rain channeled from the roof fills it again. We sympathize with her bewilder-ment, since it keeps raining, but Dry Season when it arrives, if ever it arrives, lasts a long while. We are permitted brief showers but there are five of us taking them.

Marge, practical, commonsense Marge, whose husband manages resorts so she knows about plumbing problems and water lack, finally took her by the hand and showed her Jaime laboriously filling the tub on the roof of the Men's Quarters, which provides their shower water. (Unwarned, Bob drank some of this one day, or used it to brush his teeth, and was brutally ill.) There is a washtub under the Main House we may use, Marge told our little lady. Sparingly, only if your clothes become unendurably muddy. But since nothing ever dries—she pointed to the lines strung under the house laden with shirts, underwear, towels—why bother?

This lecture helped explain the outhouse.

Its door is narrow. At night this frames a wealth of stars above the pointed pines. During the day parrots and stub-billed seed-eaters forage in the shrubs beyond the fence. The dun females are hard to tell from the Thick-billed species, so this is a challenge (if no one is waiting for me to vacate.) As is trying to spot the brown, striped, big-headed basilisks when they cease flicking on and off fallen tree boles, moving through the broken twigs and leaf litter. The males have finely barred sides, females are plain. Quite possibly they are stalking those lady seed-eaters, as given an opportunity they will eat eggs and young. Over the field beyond the fence, over the pines I sometimes see a White-tailed kite (now renamed the Black-shouldered. It is hard to remember all these name changes). It will hover, scrutinizing the ground for a meal. All creatures are hungry. Me too.

A woman in New York, finding a young White-tailed in a pet store, bought it and had it flown down to Everglades National Park, thinking it native to that area, which it isn't; she had it confused with the Swallow-tailed. I expect it was too young to differentiate. John Ogden, now National Audubon's Condor and Wood Stork and Crocodile Specialist, but then just a lowly assistant biologist, raised it. Fred Truslow and I photographed it. Bill McVaugh made a stunning painting from our photographs. I have a print of this hanging in my kitchen—hovering in my kitchen. It causes a lot of comment. It is a spectacular bird. It used to be common in the Point Lobos area of California along the Carmel River, then for years it disappeared. When I reported to the rangers that a pair hovered over the artichoke fields outside my sister's window while I ate breakfast they politely disbelieved me, so I invited them for eggs and coffee too, and showed them. The artichoke fields are long gone but the birds are back, abundant all the way up the Peninsula, and in fields north of San Francisco Bay.

The floor of this useful building—I was talking about outhouses, remember? Only I stray into birds all the time. Well, they are my business, it's hard not to. The floor is tiled in white linoleum, an unusual feature if you will search back over your memories (if you have any). The linoleum was liberated by a British officer who helped Diane build her house. To balance this artistic touch the men's biffy has a turtle painted on its seat, which is cracked. I discovered this fact one day when I had been left behind, Cinderella in the kitchen, and invaded the men's territory looking for reading material. Their quarters were neat as a pin, far more so than our ladies'. Two of those men are excellent cooks, too, and a third is willing to help with dishes, sanitizing them with boiling water, which is more than Maria and I do. Perhaps my granddaughters are on to something, insisting on equal labor by the sexes in the home. Brad was a good cook, taking over much of it on our fishing trips; also convincing me that a nightime mouse highway over my camp pillow was nothing to be distressed by. (I'm not sure how he did that. Love works miracles.) All this equality business, as I see it, is a matter of who has the time, or who is earning the groceries. My generation was raised by male Victorian standards, or at least I was. The extent of my Dad's cooking was burning waffles on Sunday when the real cook had gone to early Mass and my mother, smart woman, lay abed. Smells and language from the kitchen were equally smoky, as I remember. But who am I to criticize, I burn everything too. I just take this for granted and leave the windows open.

No such frippery as seats painted with turtles in my grandmother's three-holer! This was set in a bower of fragrant privet, a social gathering place for us children and our five maiden aunts. Grandmother was aging, winters in the old whaling town of Sag Harbor on Long Island were cold. I couldn't have been six, but I clearly remember the celebration when my father prospered sufficiently to install indoor plumbing for her. This was done at the head of the steep stairs, the throne visible to anyone coming to the front entrance if we children forgot to close the bathroom door. Perhaps Grandmother, in her pride and gratitude, wanted it that way?

As clearly I remember when our boys first encountered an outhouse. We were driving them to summer camp. In those days there were few gas stations or eateries in backwoods Canada. City children, they came dashing back from behind a roadside grocery shaken, gallantly protective (probably that's why I remember) of my femininity. They urged me back into the car. No, no bear or porcupine, they admitted—just that this was no facility for their *mother!* As they grew older, hitchhiked about the country, they learned the various animals that make a study of these backyard buildings so instructive to a naturalist. Diane tells me she once encountered a pig in one . . .

On the eastern seaboard from Gloucester, Massachusetts, where I used to visit summers, to the fishing camps in the backwoods of Florida (in those days Florida had backwoods) outhouses were adventurous, rickety structures at the ends of piers. The tides sloshed in and out below them over barnacled rocks, seaweed, the accepted trash and broken fishpots of harbors. Fish were not being diseased and rotted then (that we knew of) by the offal and pollution of cities towed out to ocean dumps.

The worst biffy I have ever had to use I will omit mentioning out of respect to the worthy organization I was working with. Besides, I don't want to remember it, nor the day an unhappy woman—never mind. She was overweight. So am I. The best was on a ranch in Virginia in a year of severe drought. Since the drought was hoped to be temporary, an original farmers' convenience was set close by the kitchen steps, complete with an oriental rug, a standing lamp, a bookshelf, ashtrays, and, as I remember, an oil painting. My favorite story about one is how Brooke Worth, studying spiders, mosquitoes, monkeys, and other fauna for the Rockefeller Foundation in Bush Bush Forest, Trinidad, was frustrated in his search for *Arachnicorus,* a spider-affiliated bug. One day, in the dimness of his latrine, well bedizened with spider webs and creepy crawlies, he realized that daily he was associating in intimate quarters with these almost-unknown-to-science objects of his search. Brooke is a dear. He hasn't written many books of his adventures in the public health field, but each one is a classic, a treasure trove of amusement even if you don't know—like me—the difference between an orb and a web.

Still Day 9. Evening
Letter to My Children

Twenty-one years ago tonight. So long ago now that perhaps in another foreign land, a full moon reflected again like an elongated lantern in water, friends about me, finally I can take out those days and look at them; perhaps even write about them so their weight will not so heavily lie inside of me any longer. They are not a cancer—just a weight, a sadness, a wonder, lying leaden. So long ago that that woman with the dancing feet skipped her way each evening between the flower beds, across the wooden walk that led to a dining room where a marimba band played gayly. There is no guilt—we do not dictate the way we are made, the astonishing actions that spring from our subconscious. Half a dozen of us were birding at Lago Atitlan, a small, shining expanse of blue in the Guatemalan Sierra, green-clad mountains steep about it, volcanoes at the far end. Reeds edged its shores between the Mayan villages.

Mornings no wind ruffled the blue surface. The primitive boat of a fisherman drifted here and there, a waterbird trailed its wake, ducks swam below the balconies of the Hotel Tzanjuyu for pieces of a breakfast roll tossed to them. In the afternoons the chucomeel wind blew in from the Pacific, carrying moisture, swirling a doughnut of cloud around the tip of the highest volcano, breaking waves onto the pebbled beaches; fisherboats were drawn up into the reeds.

In the tower room of the hotel, carried there by the Guatemalan servants, shoulders strong under their woven jackets, their eyes soft with sympathy, your father lay dying. Oxygen tanks sent over the mountains from the Embassy in the City stood by his bed. His mask . . . his heavy breathing. . . . His hand—that beloved hand—lay slack on the bed cover, reaching out to where I crouched on the floor beside him. There was no question about his future. It had been in the eyes of the two American doctors—fortuitous arrivals at this highland inn. As a favor to our leader they had examined their countryman. Now they stood outside in the corridor with me, hesitant to speak.

"Tell me!" I think I beat on the chest of the nearest one. Surely my voice did. "I have to know! I can't stand this, tell me the truth!"

They told me.

"How long?" They told me.

The mountains between us and a hospital were too high for his transport, and even if they were not it was useless. Perhaps now, with all that is known about hearts? It might have been different? They stood with me. Decent, kindly men.

I had to eat. If I were not to break I had twice a day to leave that tower room, for however short a time. Your father understood. He was conscious, just . . . far away. So in my pretty vacation dresses at breakfast and at dinner I crossed the lawn to the dining room, people smiling at me, inviting me to sit with them. I smiled back and passed on to sit with the manager's young American wife, who knew my circumstances. Each evening as I crossed on that wooden walk the music of a marimba band would drift through the lighted open windows to meet me. My world collapsing, the rock on which my life—your lives—is founded drowning in a steadily rising sea, my feet would start tripping. They danced on their toes. My skirt swayed and lilted to the music like a girl's. The day's new crop of tourists smiled at the happiness of my feet and I smiled back— two women in one body. One dead, frozen, numb; one a girl gay, alive, *dancing*. How do you explain that?

The night your father died the band did not play, the manager had known more than I did. My feet lifted on the boardwalk, stuttered, stopped in puzzlement.

"That's funny," I said to our son, who, no passport, no money, no ticket or time when my appeal reached him, had arrived. "A marimba band plays every night for dinner. It's marvelous. I wonder what has happened?"

My feet queried me again. I learned later that the manager had canceled the band out of respect. I wish he hadn't. Your father would have liked leaving to music. Silence is forever.

Twenty years ago. I could never tell you about it: you could never ask me. The weight of our silence lies within me again tonight, sitting on a porch so far from you, in a rain forest. Just as on our pond here, the lights there had shimmered on the still waters of Atitlan. The clouds there had been pink and gold in the afterglow. Our feet had rung hollowly on the boardwalk.

That night I slept across the hall in the room our leader had used. It had not been made up. He was a good friend, but there was no comfort in his cold bed. In the dark, on the fringe of consciousness, I woke to a deliberate, synchronous tread of feet in the corridor; passing with heavy finality, fading into the ultimate silence.

Years later, in Washington, sleeping in a row house with brick walls ordinarily soundproof, I was wakened, heard in the night that same heavy tread of feet. I didn't need to be told next day that my neighbor was gone.

Twenty years ago tonight. A lifetime. It has taken me a lifetime to be willing to listen again to that silence, to lake waves lapping on shale, to that heavy tramp of feet in the corridor. There is more you might ask me. You can read between the lines, but this is at least a beginning. I have lived through these years like a tree that appears normal, standing straight, its roots deep, sheltered from the wind by others growing around it; but inside hollow, burned black and dry by lightning. Tentatively once or twice I sent out green shoots, but they withered.

Over the years two men you don't know helped me. One brutal, refusing sympathy, roughly taught me to be tough, that no one helps you but yourself. He forced me to stand on my own feet. The other, meeting me later, took for granted that I was alive, and normal. He was sometimes rough too, but he nourished me, pushed me into accomplishment. I had to feel that if he believed in me I must have value. He died. He and your father would have liked each other. I think of them somewhere in that airy expanse of sky where the spirit goes when the mortal body releases it. They are sitting about a table, one with his pipe, one with a cigar. Your Uncle Jack is there, too, and Gramp, highballs in hand, looking down in amusement at my efforts, pleased with my small triumphs; waiting for me.

Does this make any sense to you? Does it explain why I have lived apart from you all, not clinging, not acting the traditional, conventional mother and grandmother? I was too easily hurt, too desperate for love. I love you, you love me, but you didn't want me sitting about your living rooms. You have had your own lives to live, your own unhappinesses to conceal.

Looking at friends of my generation I wonder if in human relations there *is* such a thing as the conventional, traditional parent or grandparent. I think they exist only as figments of the imaginations of novelists and idealists.

When you really need someone, when you stand on the outer edge of darkness, there is no one there but you. It is up to you.

Day 10

This morning I spend arguing with my flashlight, which the new bulb and batteries haven't cured, and arguing with Diane's manuscript. Who am I to think I know better than its author? Just her putative audience, I tell her. I like color and flowers and background, need people spelled out. She is a psychologist, an action person. We wrangle cheerfully. We also wrangle over whether today is Wednesday or Thursday. What does it matter in this never-never land?

We are perched on a table, slicing vegetables. The morning is young, stretches before us. We fall into a discussion of the methods and mental equipment of writers and authors, classifications that we differentiate.

My book is a journal, at the bottom of the heap, I claim. All I need do is describe the activities and feelings of one person—myself. Easy. No intellectual demands. A whodunit author—that's Diane—is a cut above this. She must build a story line, people it with characters who both feel and act, must manipulate them. This takes imagination, work. Those serious naturalist authors I run into to my great good fortune, among whom I turn speechless and humble . . .

"Pooh," says Diane. "They are just people. They leave crumbs on the table, are cranky in public with their wives."

"Never mind," I argue back. "When they write first of all they have to know their subjects in all their facets; then manipulate these in ways that attract interest; then write their information with clarity and grace. This demands intellect. It also *commands* intellect, from the reader. At its height it is scholarship clothed in poetry. I will clean up their crumbs anytime."

At a party with journalists or factual writers I am comfortable enough. With those who are naturalists to their toenails, who serve up their facts in phrases that paint in beauty, roll off the ear in music, I am quiet, dumb with happiness at being admitted to their world. I read their sentences slowly, savor the shapes of their words, hate to turn their last pages. Their volumes live on a special bedside shelf, have a special corner in my living room.

Diane is less impressed by these. Facts are what she wants, she doesn't care that much about philosophy, about presentation. And if no two people, all of whom share the same basic bone structure, look alike, she points out, neither are their mental arrangements similar, and so never will their books be alike.

"Not even whodunits?" I query. "Drugstore romances?"

No. Each of us uses our equipment differently. "Look how you hold that paring knife," she says, laughing at me. "It's a wonder your thumb isn't cut to ribbons."

We two amateur philosophers set our vegetables in the fridge and go about our work—Diane's ten uncut fingers to light that balky stove, mine to poke the keys of her balky typewriter.

. It is a sultry day, humid, overcast, hot. The group is becoming a little sultry too, novelty is wearing off. There are too many of us for the work, quarters are crowded. With the nets now twenty miles away we leave in the dark, come back in the dark; there is no time to sort out possessions and dispositions. Small selfishnesses begin to emerge, impatience. But we are a civilized group, used to travel, to adjusting. We need only think of daily routines back home, the weather we are being spared, to resume our good natures. That a night's sleep restores a lot of bounce is evident at the breakfast table. The practical and inventive set up sun and rain shelters in the forest. Photographers and song recorders endlessly fiddle with equipment. Botanists collect. The restless prowl net lanes, slide down muddy banks to swim in the river. Hard-core bird-watchers disappear, then return in worry that they may have missed seeing some rare bird in the net.

Important on any trip, our food is excellent and ample. Today instead of demolishing the usual luncheon basket of peanut butter and cheese and cold meat and (if you can get there first) leftover chicken salad, cookies, those big bananas, ripe as we can never buy them up north, it has been decided to go to that Chinese restaurant in Belmopan for lobster salad and beer. Hardly a starvation diet!

I have stayed home again to make one less body in the over-weighted cars, one less person standing about the work table. Yesterday I spent in and out of Belmopan with Dora, selecting vegetables of interesting shapes and colors while we waited for the telephone company to open its doors. We visited a Commissioner's wife—French, her home cool, her Coke a delicious gift, her rooms full of Indian artifacts. I have been in India, we could trade stories. We were retrieving our evening's meat from her refrigerator—everyone helps everyone in one way or another here; with loans of gasoline or equipment, refrigerator space, errands in the City. What a variety of living must go on in the small, identical houses! Beyond the Commissioner's double house with its fence was a tiny bookshop I'd love to get into, directly across the street from that the cement of the Market Square with its all of six shops.

Belmopan was hacked out of jungle ten years ago, into a tract of copycat houses set unimaginatively in a grid. Originally painted a dark brown, gradually the homes are being individualized, hibiscus and fruit trees and tropical vines hiding their sameness, colored doors, fences added.

One had the shield of the Venezuelan Consulate above its door—a doll house imitation of the formality of Diplomat Row on Massachusetts Avenue in Washington. I became instantly homesick. How far away in time those days when I clicked my gloved, high-heeled way into the bustle and elegance of diplomatic receptions as equally similar in planning, as equally variegated in appurtenances as these tract houses! The Russians had the most opulent food. I told Dora about it. Lush trays of colored drinks, usually oversweet and sticky; sculptures of ice flanked by piles of fruits and meats and caviar and sandwiches on ceremonial cloths accented by silver, by candles reflecting in the frosty ice. My hand being kissed—we both glanced at our hands as they are now, working hands, and laughed. I had to learn to hold food only in my left, to eat only in small bites so my mouth wasn't full when some dignitary bore down on me. I drove a Volkswagen Bug in those days—my very first own car. Brad loved me for it, he always used it for parties. It was so small, a scarlet impertinence among the long black limousines with their liveried drivers, that the police let us fit it in anywhere, right by the gates, so we could arrive late and leave early. I would squeeze Brad's arm on our way up the walks, excited at the social whirl I would be stepping into. He would squeeze mine coming out, pleased to be going home for a quiet evening in his big chair. He carried a heavy load. It killed him. Dora knows about that, too.

All this from a small Venezuelan shield on a small house in a jungle.

Day 11

We are moving the nets again, to a Park near Belmopan. Off we go after breakfast, poles, cartons, table, plant press, everything on the roofs that can be lashed. Personal equipment on laps, springs sagging, spirits high. At the end of the Old Highway, at the big mud hole doors fly open, everyone flies out. The cars charge up the rise, we pack in again. Teacher Dora talks loudly above the rattles in our car, points out changes in soil where a line of trees delineates this. We are to work in a gallery forest on the alluvial overflow of the Sibun River (well, I think it is the Sibun, I don't have my geography entirely straight). When it rains the storybook limestone hills send their burden down the river, spread it along the edge, enriching magnificent trees we now park our cars under. We are to find different species in this different vegetation.

Tropical forests are rich in bird life because fruit or flower is always in season, attracting insects, providing nectar, scattering seeds. Not only residents can be accommodated but migrants from the north, which, after all, spend seven or more months of their year in the south. We worry more and more these days about these tropical forests so vital to human life as well as wildlife. The rate of destruction taking place is incredible. By the end of this century it is calculated that half of the earth's remaining rain forests will be gone, 25 percent of the plants and animals. Latin America alone has lost more than 37 percent. When we worry we might think what *we* did to the hardwood forests of our country as population along the eastern seaboard swelled, settlers and their axes pushed west. We can't talk holier than thou. Botanists, mammalogists, lepidopterists, especially climatologists, and even thoughtful politicians are paying more attention to this destruction, not only south of our borders, but worldwide.

Ornithologists have found that "our" birds that south of the United States feed on fruits either move on to more rewarding habitats when these are consumed or turn to insects and grain. When Dry Season dries up these resources their gizzards readapt as fruit reappears. Catbirds will come to feeders there for cracked corn, as quail and song sparrows do here in the north. Redstarts hawk like flycatchers, have even evolved broad bills for this. Tennessee and Cape May warblers seek out nectar. The changes are fascinating—and frightening. When the forests are gone will they live? Will we live?

At the Park all is confusion. Nets are being stretched and tightened, troublesome shrubbery hacked away. The first birds caught hang in their colored bags, waiting to be processed. Ponchos are stretched over the work table against a drizzle. Dave is coaxing a bird into position in his box, complaining about the light. I slip off to the River; I would just be in the way.

I find—out with my notebook—a pair of Green kingfishers with white-dotted wings that fly like arrows above the current, diving for minnows. A wintering waterthrush bobs on the muddy verge, flicking its tail, flicking leaves aside with its bill. Warblers dart and hover at different levels. Which ones where? In the heavier branches, on the trunk? Out on the tips? I make notes. This is how birds coexist, not impinging on the food supplies of another species. My perch is comfortable, trees fend off a gentle rain. I have dealt, at home, with my annual reports, my IRS forms, the Christmas mail. That home is far away, probably drifted with snow. Not until I wish need I leave this quiet spot, return to the banding table, report on the kingfishers, which may be life birds for some.

When I do I find we have acquired guests, in company of the Prime Minister's sister, a small woman who has done a large amount to promote conservation in her country. Between them she and Dora have worked political miracles. I know her best as a warm-hearted woman who always gives me a fine hug and who has a special hummingbird in her City yard. I used to walk from our hotel evenings to hunt it. Belize is small, the Prime Minister's compound was only a block away, along a curving street where storm waves crested the waterfront wall. No luck on the hummers usually, but Meg would be there, call me in from her window.

The guests leave. Dora decides she and I should go shopping, Belmopan is just beyond the Park. We stop by the open market, pick over bananas, tomatoes, and vegetables strange to me, starchy roots fat to look at and doubtless fattening. We fill cartons we have brought for the purpose, I lug them back to the car.

Coffee, says Dora firmly, leading me to a counter in a sort of tent at the back. Smells and smoke rise from hot oil in skillets. Probably Dora has had no breakfast. She is always up early but I rarely see her sitting at table.

Coffee comes in a paper cup. Rings of dough are spattered into a skillet—the local version of doughnuts? Dora puts one on my napkin. It is greasy, sprinkled with sugar. She is more used to these and enjoys them more than I do.

We drive to the supermarket on the other side of town—
that means across a street and down a block. I find this ram-
bling structure nearly empty both of goods and people. Flour
and sugar and such are at one end, hardware, lightbulbs—we
need some, I head that way and ah! find flashlight batteries—
at the other. Yeast is sold at the Cheese Corner where a woman
sits surrounded by paper packages and large, mysterious bot-
tles. One of these she picks up to satisfy my order. I wish a
pound? (Have you any idea how much a *pound* of yeast would
be?) A half-pound? And she wants to do this in *grams!* Bored
by my indecision, she pours granules into a plastic bag until I
think there is enough to satisfy the culinary demands on my
time for the next two weeks. Then, remembering my promise
to make cinnamon rolls, that this work crew is shortly to leave,
unknown appetites will replace them, I recklessly double the
amount. I can always take the extra home. Yeast doesn't harbor insects, and once Diane is rid of us I doubt she cooks again
for months. Not bread, certainly. While appreciative, she hasn't
exactly hung over my shoulder as I pour oats, bran, cornmeal,
raisins, flour, whatever I can poach from her shelves into the
big dishpan they lend me for mixing.

At the gas station a man tinkers awhile with our car's
plumbing. We check out the banding crew. A lot of mopping
is in progress. Rain has filled our protective poncho roof with
ponds, they spill through onto the record sheets. But cameras
and lunch, binoculars and books have been stowed under the
table, the air is warm, between showers birds fly, a few get
caught, no one seems unhappy. So we check out Jaime, chop-
ping future net lanes down Hummingbird Highway on the
other side of Belmopan, and go home. I am Off Duty. Don't
be rude and ask me when I was On. Someone has to lug the
vegetables . . .

I close the windows, carelessly left open in Diane's house,

move the beds further in, read, wash my hair, borrow the typewriter, inspect the evening's fragrant stew. What vacation could offer more? Well—dry clothing, but I ignore this dream. I have grown used to living permanently damp.

Later

Marge comes in laughing, to report she was bitten by a Brown jay. As an old hand this didn't bother her, but the tyros worry, surprised we don't carry disinfectant with us. Both Marge and I get questions at banding demonstrations we give about being bitten, scratched, and punctured, the dangers. Don't birds carry diseases? Well, yes, they do. As do humans, far more dangerously. I have handled birds for how long? More than thirty years, and while screech owls, which I rarely catch, tear my fingers as I work at extricating theirs, and pelican and Black-backed gulls from polluted waters rip my wrists, I have never had any real injury. A cardinal or grosbeak can raise a blood blister on even my tough fingers, but you learn (rapidly) to hold them so they don't. A hawk, which can rip apart a rabbit or furry rodent with its hooked bill, is only dangerous if it sinks its talons into you. I don't wear gloves to handle them, just go at them carefully with as little tension as I can muster, so that they too are not tense. The trick with hawks is to grasp their legs from the rear. The trick with pelican is to grasp their bills. The trick with gulls is to get them between your knees as fast as you can. I haven't handled many big hawks, except a caracara once that was docile as a hen, but maybe I have just been lucky. Sharpshins and kestrels, which are small, have grabbed me, but with them I am more careless.

Their talons are sharp, and hurt, but not too much. Besides, I am hurting them—their pride—so of course they strike at me. In self-defense. A kingfisher's bill is serrated, the better to hold slippery fish. When one of these holds my finger it is really difficult to pry that heavy bill open. If no one is around to help I have to play a game of patience. Last winter, an unusually cold one on Cape Cod, a flock of crows came boldly to my doormat for corn kernels. We eyed each other through the glass door, and I wondered how I might perhaps take them in a trap. My nets would never hold one; crows are mighty smart. They like oranges. In the spring when I set these out for orioles arriving hungry from Mexico, needing sweets, the crows swoop in and steal them. They clean out citrus rinds in my compost heap, too; they also must have a sweet tooth. They are so bold and brassy I find it hard not to admire them. When they pluck tern chicks and long-legged baby plovers off the beaches where I do my studies, and mockingbird babies out of nests in my neighbors' trees, I feel differently.

Still Day 11

I have a letter I brought south with me to answer. A woman has requested "a few words" on my experiences with Cabin Fever, a disease she feels I must be subject to. She is writing a series for a magazine that might be interesting; I'd like to learn how other people cope with isolation. An article on Cabin Fever is probably as useful to the world as a bird banded, never encountered again, the band lost in hawk or cat droppings. One of my bands was reported once, picked up on a beach with a gull's long-dead leg attached to it. A woman in need of natural food to feed an injured owl once retrieved a catbird dead in the highway, smack on the Florida-Georgia border. I had banded it.

What can I say to this woman? For what it is worth here is my reply, written on the verandah this morning. I will remodel it on Diane's typewriter. My letters may sound as if I dash them off in a hurry, but really they are the result of respectable effort. I have a friend who brings me books on grammar. I don't know why he remains a friend, except he also brings me wine and has an affectionate smile.

"Dear Correspondent:

I don't have your magazine at hand, partly because I am in Central America, partly because often I bundle my magazines to give to students working on a barrier beach, living without the amenities of electricity, radio, plumbing, reading material, and—more important—privacy. I do remember being jealous that your protagonist had a loving man to live and talk with and to unload her frustrations on.

"I am spending my septuagenarian years,—well, I haven't lived through them all yet—making surveys of birds on wildlife preserves not yet studied. Since ornithological research is done best where there are no cats or dogs for company, no disturbance by neighbors, hunters, ranchers, visitors, I have had plenty of opportunity to develop cabin fever, but alas, I can't help you, for I never did.

"I lived in solitude. Once I had a telephone, but it operated only out, not in. I was never in to hear it. The women in our city office, not knowing this, worried I had broken an ankle, been struck by a rattlesnake, but I never was. Once I was seventeen miles from my rural delivery mailbox, over a road impassable in rain, which gives you an idea of my isolation.

Once I was fifteen dusty miles from a one-room post office general store with irregular hours. It was always closed when I took time to drive to it. It also was inaccessible in rain; I had to cross a broad river wash subject to flash flooding. Once I was seventy-five miles from anywhere. My mail accumulated in the city until someone brought it to me, navigating a final ten miles of desert and creek beds to do so. My short-wave radio brought in foreign countries but only in foreign languages and of course was only one-way, so I couldn't alert the Baptists in Ecuador or the Japanese or Germans when I encountered a rattlesnake or ran out of eggs.

"Once I had shifted my social gears I found these solitudes marvelous. While I grumbled to my sponsors of The Nature Conservancy about loneliness, weather, the lack of mountain lions and the birds I had hoped to record, I wouldn't have missed a moment of it. On one ranch I did have a friend for company. She was first-rate at making our recalcitrant stove and our jeep perform, which I never could have done. As her idea of diet was nuts and raisins, and I enjoy cooking, I was glad to forgo my solitude. Another location was accessible, by which I mean I could see my car from where I slept, although it took my tenderfoot nervousness an hour and a half to drive the thirty-one miles to civilization—if the road was dry. A pleasant young manager was in charge of me there but rarely present. He left me his puppy to care for, a passel of cats that cared for themselves (and ate the birds I was studying), an assortment of horses, cattle that had broken through fences, and three burros that occasionally came visiting down the road. Catching birds in mist nets scattered among these various companions posed problems but enlivened my landscape.

"So you see I have had plenty of opportunity to suffer from cabin fever. I was too busy coping with each day, or enjoying what I was doing, to develop it. Maybe my trouble with answering your questions is that I *like* isolation. Or have I just learned to accept it, out of necessity? I wouldn't know."

People who request "a few words" from me get into more than they expect.

I lay aside my pencil and soak up the noon peace. Solitude nourishes me, the world is timeless when I am alone. A slow drift of clouds, light changing as our planet turns, a lizard that scampers up a vine, looks about, is gone in an eye wink—these are important to me. Down on the bare drive Maria has scattered seeds. Small doves feed there, arguing over her bounty. Across the lawn their bigger cousins sit quietly in the pines. Little birds move restlessly about them. A really large dove, the Pale-vented pigeon, perches like a Christmas ornament on a pine tip, its mate close by. Unlike the big doves of Florida and the Caribbean, whose cooing was a constant obbligato to my hours, these are silent: I am aware of them only from the whoosh of their heavy flight, the shaking of a branch as they settle. This scene must have existed through the stretch of past time, and it will continue—if we can learn to care for our world—far into the future. Lightning and fire will blacken, lumbering erode, but the green regenerates. Man with his restlessness and hunger, his craving for change, activity, accomplishment, destroys his indolent Edens. But the green regenerates, the birds and animals return.

The dogs lift their heads, growl. A truck rolls up to the gate, our canine guardians race, barking, lunging at the fence. Maria appears. After much calling back and forth in patois a package is left, the truck departs. Obviously offended by the residue of its exhaust, still growling, the dogs go off to circle their boundaries, to investigate more natural smells. The texture of my morning has been torn. I set my letter aside. Maria fetches the package, busies herself in the kitchen clattering tableware, leaves for her home. I replace her. There is always housework for women to do.

I have lived alone for twenty years (on some days I can detail the months, too). Once I had broken away from our home, where the sense of loss was a total absence of sunlight, an encircling fog, I learned, slowly, to adjust to solitude: a solitude of the spirit, anyway. Being crowded on a bench, an arm around my waist at a party, merry chatter, an affectionate kiss— these are all very well, but too sustained they make me nervous, don't give me time for myself. I don't want to move on the tide as one piece jammed into a raft of flotsam, I need to eddy at my own uncertain pace, come to rest on a sandbar or a mudflat where fiddler crabs scuttle. Living with this group in Belize, I find I withdraw to my bed with a book, or into my evening corner, letting the bustle and cheer go on about me but without me.

I am not the only one. There is that woman who sits alone at meals, the man who goes off—"exploring," he apologizes. Not for long, for he carries his share of the work, but he needs, however briefly, solitude. Diane withdraws on afternoon walks or into her room, where the door is always closed. I must go in to fetch her typewriter, its space is cluttered with household goods moved from their normal spots to accommodate us. Her bed is a mattress on the floor, she must have trouble getting to it! But in there she is invisible, as Dora makes herself, in her bathroom. This latter looks, from the doorway, normal. Books, household supplies, and medicines are stacked on shelves. There is a toilet—only it must be flushed with a bucket of water. There is a shower, but it is fitted with a mysterious arrangement of hoses and pans. It is also the passage to her bedroom, where our handbags and valuables are shoved out of sight under a jumble of clothing, so there is frequent through traffic. As it adjoins the kitchen and our Common Room she can never be out of sound of us, but it does have a door; she can snatch a few moments of spiritual privacy.

Some people seem to have no need for solitude, seem always to want to be in a jostle. I interest myself noting the degrees. As our days pass people have sorted themselves out—the cheerful morning chatterers from those only weakly smiling after a second cup of coffee. Those who rarely talk at all, although comfortable companions. The quietly capable from the anxious flutterers, leaders from followers, the knowledgeable (whether true or false) from the questioners, the spoon-fed from investigators-on-their-own. It is fun to observe. Quiet ones blossom, noisy ones accede to the Peter Principle, rising visibly to their levels of incompetence. Without malice we tease each other, trade amused gossip on our way to and from our sleeping quarters. We will part friends, but each of us shows only the tip of an iceberg.

At dinner we help ourselves from a great kettle of stew, ladle it onto chunks of bread—every meal bread. We empty the salad bowls. Dessert is fruit, or the usual cake—tonight with a rich banana sauce from a pitcher that makes the rounds. I cut the sweetness of mine with a shot of rum, am observed, copied. Rum has become a staple, lightly blurring our evening weariness. I take a lot of ribbing for it, having produced the first bottle. We don't yet use it on pancakes, I point out, though after a rainy early-morning transect it could be suitable, warming. It is good in coffee, too, I say, splashing some in my mug. I am magnanimously sharing this bottle, bequeathed to me by the Colonel when he departed.

As the dishes pass back and forth I look about our table.

How much—and how little—shows when people are in a group, their sentences public. Arrogant, detached, gentle, aggressive—the real person is obscured by social talk. That woman always first and last in line, a chocolate eater grossly overweight, hides a bitter unhappiness told me in a rush one night when she was overwhelmed. She has a lovely singing voice, no amount of coaxing will bring it out. That one, a quiet scientist from another discipline, has a child in an institution, never mentions a husband. This new one, young, just arrived, with hair like sunlight, is pure extrovert, she turns cartwheels on the grass to vent her energy. The first time I met her, she was bound for Europe to work in an Italian zoo with a backpack, and $15 in her pocket. Henry is a photographer, preferring flowers to birds because they stay still. He can be found anytime out in the fields, waiting for sun to hit the proper angle, the wind to quiet motion. I persuaded Henry to come on this trip, we are friends from bird tours of past years. When I was so desperate in those early days after Brad's death, inconsolable, he kept quiet watch over me: when I swam too far out; if, unable to sleep, I left my cubicle nights to roam the jungle paths. Rebuked for this latter by Authority, I defended myself, explaining that I was listening for jaguar. This was at Tikal, Guatemala, when the University of Pennsylvania was excavating the great temples, long before the clearing they made in the forest miles of an ancient culture became a government Park, tourists pounding the trails into roads. I diverted my critic by telling how, quiet in the night, no wind, something had passed so closely behind me that my hair ruffled on my neck. As I pondered what it could have been—a large owl?— it had returned, soundlessly, only its wings stirring the air. Authority was not interested in nocturnal birds, snakes were his worry. He made it clear they should be mine.

Blessed Henry—he saw to it I ate my meals, knew which was my path to my room, or hut, made it safely through each day. He hasn't aged a bit; I hope he is enjoying himself. He does have a wife, and a daughter. I learned this when he wrote once asking for a photograph he could show them: he must have mentioned me once too often. I sent him one of a stocky woman in her sixties, head bent over a hawk I was holding, white hair tousled, shirttails out. Obviously not a sexual threat! En route to Florida one fall my car developed trouble conveniently near his southern town. He was pleased to see me, received me in an old-fashioned business office with rocking chairs and a rolltop desk I immediately coveted. However, he did not suggest taking me home for dinner, or putting me up overnight. I chuckled at my image as *femme fatale* as I went on my way.

I've liked a lot of the men I've traveled and worked with. The younger generations (they are plural) expect me to carry my own gear, scramble unaided into boats, help them haul these boats above the tide line. The hugs they give me are unromantic. It's better that way, I decided early; I get to more, and to more interesting, places. Although I could wish they had the old-fashioned manners. They rarely hold a door open for me, pass the jam at breakfast, or pick up my suitcases. My grandmother would cuff them.

In Florida, after being in the field all day, at first I used to put on a long skirt and a pretty blouse for dinner to remind them—and me—that I am a woman. In time I came to settle for less elegance since—being a woman—it was I who was doing the cooking while they talked shop. Nowadays, with an influx of girl biologists into the field, the men are as apt to be doing the cooking as their girls, and the girls are talking shop, being as able biologists as the men they are living with. Sometimes more able, which creates problems they bring to me.

Adjusting to their life-styles—and their language!—keeps me flexible. If she could see *my* life-style these days, Grandmother would cuff *me*.

I wrench my thoughts back from South Florida, those friendly young men now scattered about the country, silver grown into their beards. Some still surface in my life—unexpectedly at my door, no matter where it has moved to. They send me their friends to feed and bed, papers they have written, Christmas cards, Valentines, photographs of their babies.

Henry twinkles at me across the table, offers me a penny for my thoughts. He is becoming a specialist in photographing variations of eye rings and bills of the birds we catch. Never having handled birds before, he is enthralled. His eyes and mine move on to a small woman, a botanist never separated from notebook and pencil, measuring, sketching. What lies beneath the tip of her iceberg, we are all curious to know? Living in another world? Dwarfed by her husband's reputation? She has been pleasant the few times I have gone out of my way to speak with her. Shy?

I should have gone out of my way more often; this crew leaves tomorrow. We miss a lot of opportunities. Because we are shy ourselves? Too busy? Insensitive? Across my table, reaching for the banana sauce, is a small man with a white beard magnificent as his appetite. We all wonder where he stows those big second helpings, the extra plate of pancakes. I know no more of him today than when we were introduced. How *can* you eat three informal meals a day with people, cram intimately into cars with them, hang out your underpants together, and know them so little? How is it Donald Culross Peattie described us? "A handful of supple earth and long white stones with seawater running in our veins."

What informs the spirit that differentiates these?

Day 12

I am again alone on the verandah, with a book and lemonade, too indolent to make use of either. It is mid-afternoon, the thermometer reads 90° F. It is humid. Greens of leaf and grass are intense. Straight-boled pines thrust into a bowl of sky, limitless, higher than skies of the north, a pure February blue. Their candled tips toss in a breeze too high to reach me or the pond, although it rattles the big leaves of a cecropia, turns them inside out and shimmers palm fronds. As indolent as I a lone egret stands in the reeds, white against green. A duck trails triangles on the pond. The larger and more savage of the Dobermans nuzzles my chest, wanting to be kissed. It is deliciously peaceful, everyone off somewhere.

I did my good deed for the afternoon. Back at the house I turned the jeans and socks and underwear spread out on the wire fence, moved them again into the path of the sun for my co-workers. Then I had looked along Diane's shelf of books to see what it might offer and had found one she has been urging on me, on How To Get Published, by a woman who writes a weekly column for aspiring authors. I don't need to get publshed. The only book I have ever written, will ever write, is in New York (thank God) being set in proof. With its sketch of a balchatri trap. I rub my knee reminiscently, turn the pages of this one idly, find a chapter on how, for best results, to get along with your editor.

You should, writes Judith Applebaum, manage to get on personal terms with him or her as soon as possible. I chuckle. The first man to accept my book had been a friend, so we started on personal terms. He would never sit near the music in a restaurant, he couldn't keep his feet still. He was an attractive Irishman, fortunately I didn't often see him, he had a wife. He died, the manuscript went elsewhere, was accepted, reached the desk of a female editor with whom I tangled the only time I met her, and ever after over the telephone and by Uncle Sam's post. Our relations became extremely personal: I broke our contract. My current editor I promptly fell in love with (over the telephone) and became immediately as personal with as one can under that handicap, and as a reserved lady New Englander. Judith details a few gambits to try, but I bypassed those our first week. She gives advice about contracts. I must have skipped the small print on mine, if there was any. I certainly didn't wrangle over details of percentages and such with that friendly telephone voice. If he didn't know what we were doing, I was in no position to tell him. I do try to ask a few questions from time to time, to pretend I have some business sense. I may *have* to write another book, to keep him on my wire. About what? My bridge-playing friends in the north think I lead a life of glamorous excitement, dabbling in ornithology. There's a lot I don't tell them. Like going out to the biffy at 2:00 A. M. by flashlight, exploring the facilities for spiders before sitting.

To occupy my mind on this hot afternoon I wonder about editors. How do they relate to their authors, their authors to them? Do authors lean as on a parent or a psychiatrist? Do they expect to be cosseted, demand affection? Is the intimacy that grows embarrassing because, like your doctor, an editor sees your hidden weaknesses and irresponsibilities, must deal with these courteously, must conceal his knowledge? Must be careful not to let you lean, expect personal attentions out of business hours you have no right to ask? How do editors defend themselves from authors who treat them like hired help? My curiosity is boundless.

A first-rate editor (I've listened to some reminisce) must know how his authors' minds work, their egos, the degree of sophistication they bring to their writing. He must manipulate or motivate them to advantage, honey-tongue his criticisms, be hard-headed in business arrangements, be a patient listener. Is that telephone voice I talk with open and friendly because so far we have had no major difference? I feel it unfair that he knows me so well, seeing me exposed on my pages, while I can only guess at him, grasping hints as we talk from his tone, his silences. He deals gently—so far—with my ignorance, seems unhurried, is crystal-clear about business obligations. He forgets details, though (clay feet).

Greedy, I want to know what is at his end of the telephone. What is his office like? Are his feet on the desk, are there plants on his windowsill, family photographs, half-empty ashtrays and coffee cups? I think not—any space is piled with papers, and notes on the backs of envelopes, some of which have to do with me, that have never surfaced since he wrote them. He warned me of this at the time. Cheerfully. Surely there must often be someone in his office with him, another phone ringing. Does he eat a sandwich at his desk for lunch, shuffling papers, or go out to meet a woman whose eyes crinkle with pleasure as she sees him coming? His assistant is young, from her voice; also friendly. An essential, I judge, in the publishing business. She also knows where everything is—equally essential.

When we hang up am I wiped clean from their slates, or do they sometimes wonder about me as I do about them? Ours is a pleasant relationship; probably I should leave it alone. I don't think I want to meet this man. I don't want his physical appearance coming between me and that voice, that understanding of what I am stammering (because he has listened so often to similar stammering?). In person he might be elderly, in a pin-striped suit and a bow tie—I would be intimidated. He might be fat, or slovenly, or dapper. . . . OH NO! I could never feel the same about him again.

My previous editors have been mostly friends, academic types concerned with veracity rather than style. I KNEW their feet were on their desks, I GAVE them the plants on their windowsills—or at least free advice on the leggy ones they neglected. Dealing with facts, not fiction, I felt free to dispute them.

Once I drove five hundred miles to thank the editor-publisher who had rescued Richard ffrench's *Guide to the Birds of Trinidad and Tobago* after its first printing had been destroyed. Getting this *Guide* published had been my swan song, I had thought at the time, not expecting to live—my grateful gift to ornithology for what this science had given me. I had no part in its writing, I just encouraged it, collected a little data for it, pushed and hauled and shoved to get it through a publisher, whose successor then mishandled it and permitted its destruction. So when Harrowood Books found the plates, obtained the legal and other rights, waited for Richard's additions, finally—it took more than four years—released this valuable volume, I cared very much about thanking its owner in person. I knew him also only from his voice—formal, English. I envisioned him as elderly, correct, definitely wearing a pin-striped suit. I dressed myself to match this image, only by the Sunday morning I had managed to locate his home on a small country lane I was no longer as tidy or in command as I had wished, but in my usual state of fluster. This didn't matter. I found, high on an extension ladder, a six-footer in his twenties with a gorgeous mop of curly red-gold hair and beard framing the bluest of eyes, the biggest and cheeriest of grins. He had stayed home from a weekend of hang-gliding to welcome me. So much for building a man from his voice. . . . Like all publishers and editors he seems incapable of writing a letter. If I need to know if he is still alive, back from the Amazon or skin diving on a barrier reef, I must reach him by telephone. Why can't men whose business is words string a few paragraphs together, or at least hire someone to do this for them? And lick a stamp? Too busy dealing with authors like me, I guess. They come to hate the written word even if it buys their groceries.

I'm not sure I would get along with a lady editor; she might be bossy. The one I had was a bitter experience. She liked her ideas and words better than mine, we parted company. I did have another, in London, who accepted a paper of mine by return air mail, requesting photographs. Naturally we got along! Only she died.

I suppose, I think regretfully, finishing my lemonade while the Doberman licks my ear, editors come in as many shapes and kinds and temperaments as their writers—or as the birders I have promised cookies for dinner, so I had better make them. Diane is taking a nap to rest her tired feet. But it has been fun thinking about them (editors), hearing the voices I knew in past years from Florida, California, Maine. Just the right amount of effort for a ninety-degree afternoon.

Day 13. Day of Departure for Crew No. 1

At 8:00 A. M. luggage is piled under the verandah against rain. We are piled there, too, awaiting the van to take our travelers to the airport. Have I said (well, only once or twice a day) that in this country roads are narrow and pot-holed? That with a 95 percent duty on new cars, the old ones are driven to the point of complete collapse? The possibilities of flat tires, breakdowns, accidents are probabilities. There are no roadside mechanics. Driving the sixty miles to the airport demands an allowance of ample time.

At 8:30 there is still no sound of the van chugging down our road. The young woman who walks over with her dogs and from time to time brings us fresh bread also takes radio messages for us. Delivered from time to time, casually, with the bread. She knows about today's van and its importance. At 8:45 Dora tears off in the rusted, sagging Chevrolet she no longer trusts to see what can be learned.

It is plenty. The young woman had a visitor the night before, a mechanic of sorts who thought to improve her radio's reception, left it on the wrong frequency. So this morning the van's owner was unable to get through to say his vehicle was inoperable. When Dora reached him he had sent two taxis out as replacements, but one had broken down, both had returned to the city to obtain a second replacement. When they might arrive—or if—was anyone's guess. Quite probably not in time to reach a plane that always has a line of eager standbys.

For once visibly alarmed, Dora herds our travelers into her cars. Certainly one of these, probably both, are short of gas; we did a lot of driving yesterday. Don't be silly, of course the gauges don't work, although Dora's windshield wiper unexpectedly, inexplicably has started to function. We offer up a prayer to St. Christopher, wave farewell. If they take the shortcut they won't meet the taxis coming out, but time is urgent. Send the taxis back by the shortcut, is Dora's final order. Just in case.

Note: They made the airport, they made their plane; delayed. They made Miami. Every airport in the eastern United States was closed that weekend by blizzards. Have you ever seen the Miami Airport in an emergency? People sit on the floor on normal days! We heard from one man; he had reached New Jersey three days later. By way of Chicago.

I know only too well the strain of getting overseas guests to overseas airports. A few winters ago—I have never been the same since—I had to run the Asa Wright Nature Centre in Trinidad, which is really just an inn, for six weeks. Six terrible weeks. It was midwinter, every room full, thirty guests, more, I didn't have time to count them as they came and went. I had gone down for an Annual Meeting, stayed for a few days after the other Trustees left. While I was at the other end of the island, the manager walked out, leaving behind him a panicked staff—two excellent cooks, one of whom gave notice; three young maids about whom the less said the better, and who, being shy, spoke only in whispers; and those in patois. A receptionist-housekeeper who tiddled, I shortly discovered.

The one outside man, "the plantation manager," was a hold-over from Asa's day, in his late seventies (as was I). And ME, become an instant member—director—of the staff; also panicked. I was—am, although now forever in absentia—a Trustee. An Honorary Trustee, my period of service long past.

Spring Hill Plantation, as it was called in Asa's day, I wish we hadn't changed the name, had been one of my homes. Asa had taken me in after Brad's death, mothered me with her big heart and booming voice. I went back to her for years, leaning on her strength, caring for her when she had a heart attack, grieving as I watched her tragic deterioration. I had helped her dream of turning this shabby plantation with its famous Oil Bird Cave into a sanctuary. My picture hangs on the salon wall by hers—she in the gown with which she was presented at the court of St. James, me in shorts. There was no honorable way I could close the doors of her home and our Centre and walk out on this tropical paradise, become internationally famous for its birds and flowers and insects, frogs and butterflies, rain forest and mountain stream; a museum. Its rooms were booked solidly through the spring.

Dr. William Beebe—are any of you naturalists? He was also the Bathysphere Man, first to plumb the ocean depths—in his last years he was Asa's nearest neighbor, his Research Station an outpost of the New York Zoological Society. He had gone to school with my mother, whom he claimed to remember. Maybe he did; Mother was an outrageous flirt, even in her seventies, and pretty. Asa used to put the overflow of his visitors in her spare rooms, gradually adding to these as interest in tropical wildlife and birds grew and Spring Hill became a mecca for naturalists, a sort of inn. A highly informal inn! Now more formal, it was in my hands—or rather, on my shoulders. That first evening we had five plumbing emergencies. What do I know about plumbing? Only to put wastebaskets under gushing pipes, I did think of that. I had the sociable, amused sympathy of thirty guests, but not when it affected their comfort. None of them had reservations home.

There has never been any means of communication at the Centre. Uncertain mail arrives fifteen miles down a mountain road in Arima—a road built for donkey carts. Of course there was no telephone, even the one in Arima didn't work, it just looked like a phone. Messages and delayed cables went back and forth with taxi drivers, on the days when taxi drivers came to take people birding and to the airport. These must be arranged for in advance. Well in advance. Most of the drivers had been Asa's personal friends, stopping by for a chat, for tea, for an occasional job. They knew me, took me under their wings, I couldn't have functioned without them. But—

There were no medical facilities, no bellhops to carry luggage up the hill at midnight to the raw, just-added cottages where geckos frolicked on the walls, causing hysteria among citified women I ushered in by flashlight. My second day The Law arrived in the persons of two fat and angry men, the local Social Security, announcing their intent of jailing the Manager—me—for nonperformance of paperwork over years. In fifteen minutes they were laughing so hard their evil plans were forgotten, although they did leave a stack of forms for me to worry over. Everyone laughed, all those six weeks. Even arrivals who came in unexpectedly and dinnerless—once fifteen of them—at 9:00 P.M. The cooks were magnificent. Number 1 gave notice regularly, cried, stayed on when I cried too. An East Indian handyman showed up from heaven. He was a plumber and electrician willing to go into the kitchen with me in emergencies, chop carrots and tomatoes and whatever leftovers could be found in the fridge while a cook stirred up noodles with mysterious, delicious ingredients. The maids would pour rum drinks into our latecomers, the emergency would resolve. In the tropics all emergencies seem to resolve, but they take their toll from a New Englander!

Who hauled that dead and bloated dog out from under the living room one hot Sunday? A British naval officer helped, but his assistant threw up, was useless. Who carried suitcases up the hill at midnight, down at 6:00 A.M.? Pried laggard men out of their showers, shoved breakfast bananas into their still-damp hands, dispatched them to the airport; praying they wouldn't be too late, as I had no bed for them if they returned? Who, when the housekeeper drank—well, only a little, but it did interfere with her duties and left me trying to manage the maids and her front desk, act as bookkeeper in two currencies with no calculator and no mathematical skills. Try multiplying and dividing in your head by 37.7, which was the exchange at that time! I paid bills out of three checkbooks that hadn't been balanced in years. When one account bounced I switched to another. Or scooped up the Trinidad money I had collected—often inaccurately—and went to Arima, where the bank clerks ignored me because I was a woman. The American money—valuable—I stowed in a roll of old maps in an ancient armoire whose drawers wouldn't close. A lot of American money. It, and its location, bugged the eyes of my successor, who had managed the International Airport and was used to more conventional systems than mine.

I did finally get a successor. Exhausted and angry after six weeks, seeing no relief coming, I informed the local Trustees I was closing down the Centre. Come hell or high water. On Tuesday—in mid-season. I had reached the end of my strength.

It was a hilarious period. Even I laughed all day. Everyone helped. Guests did my arithmetic, set out fruit in the early mornings for the hummingbirds and tanagers they had come to photograph, reported on a nesting pair of hawks I never had time to check out. My laughter became more hollow as the weeks went on. I didn't get much sleep for worrying. At 3:00 A.M. I would be out on the gallery in my nightgown, scrutinizing by flashlight our blackboard, where plane arrivals and departures were scheduled, erased, rescheduled so often I couldn't remember the details. Making sure those trips to the airport were listed and under control, praying that drivers would show up. So, as I was saying a few pages back, I could understand Dora's tight-lipped concern about getting her charges to the airport!

I could write a book on that Trinidad experience; easily, from the hysterical letters I would write midnights and fire off to those U. S. Trustees who had left me to shoulder their burden. I begged them to come to my rescue, flattered, stormed, beseeched. No one ever answered; I was on my own. I had to wonder if they even opened my envelopes? My only help came from visiting Tour Directors, efficient people accustomed to trouble. Some of them, when our New York office overbooked us, had to sleep on the extra bed in my room. But if I lost these as friends—Tour Directors, who are tired and need privacy, and the Trustees, who didn't answer their mail—I made lots of new ones. About thirty a week, all hungry, all enjoying the Centre and my dilemmas. My special memories are of a German baritone, no English, who sang opera every night at dinner, to thank me for standing (for hours) in line at the Arima Post Office to buy stamps for him to send to his collector friends at home. Well, what is a Manager's job but to keep her guests happy? Those two cooks are enshrined in my heart. My tiddly housekeeper—her condition was clear at meals when she would embrace me, saying over and over to our embarrassed guests, "Mrs. Fisk, she is FANTASTIC." Looking about at the happy faces, at the laden buffet table, at the roof not—at the moment—leaking, probably a little tiddly myself as a hard day drew to its end, I would have to agree with her. However reluctantly.

Day 14

I am on the verandah—gallery, they call it in tropical countries; I don't know why. Its swinging couch, heavy wooden chairs, its railing edged with sansevieria recall the porches of many an Adirondack resort. Slowly I finish the salad I made for lunch, sip a fruit drink from the shelf Diane keeps full in the fridge. We have no ice.

I am regarding intently the man who, having carried his salad plate into the kitchen, is now reading. Staring is really what I am doing, only staring has a rude connotation. My gaze is wholly friendly, affectionate. I am watching the sunlight that flicks off the leaves, slides down his cheekbones; the movement of his eyes—hazel, with flecks of gold, I decide—across the paper in his hands; the occasional twitch of his mouth. His hair is brown, curly, well cut. His clothes are well cut too, an enjoyable contrast to our old T-shirts and jeans. I study his hands, square, well kept, clean—goodness, how clean! I tuck mine out of sight. We don't have hot water for scrubbing here.

He looks up, questioning, eyebrows raised. "I am just looking at you," I say. "Does it make you nervous? I've waited so long to see you, I need so much to know what you look like, who you really are behind those manuscripts we trade."

He marks his place and looks across at me, equally assessing, equally affectionate. He is not nervous. He is a man comfortable with himself, comfortable in his job. Although we have worked together for more than a year, we have not met before; he arrived by taxi early this morning. I know him only from correspondence, from notes on the margins of our pages, from an occasional telephone call. He is orderly, meticulous in detail, with a clarity of mind I despair to emulate. He is also good-humored and humorous, patient. I, who am nervous with almost everyone, hiding what matters to me, have never been nervous with him, never once tried to hide since that day when he called and requested my collaboration. He gave no flattery, made no effort at manipulation. My astonished acceptance sprang from the timber of his voice—sensitive, vigorous, male. I trusted him immediately.

"Why?" I asked him months later, when the question would come too late to disrupt our relationship. We were having one of our rare long-distance calls. "With all those students you have trained, whose abilities you knew, how did you happen to pick on me?"

He had laughed his warm laugh. "I'd read your articles, I'd asked about you. Besides, I once wrote you for information. I liked the way you handled it, so I gambled."

I remembered. Some years ago on plain paper he had requested a copy of research I had done for the government. Thinking him a schoolboy I had answered brusquely, inquiring whether his interest was in the abbreviated version; in the pages that applied to his area only; or in the complete report, which ran to some sixty pages. If the latter it would be copied at his expense, I wrote tartly, and the postage charged to him. In spring I often get requests of this type from students casting about vaguely for a summer project. "Please send me all you know about . . ." Usually my reference to money silences them.

On official stationery he had replied promptly, enclosing a check. Pleased with his wording I had returned the overage, explained my brusqueness, forgotten the incident. Now we look at each other comfortably, remarking on how fortuitous life can be.

He has interrupted a trip to South America to stop here, to bring me in person a copy of our current chapters. You don't dare mail anything important to these countries. Besides, he says, his eyes amused, *he* wanted to see what *I* am really like, to fit me into those disorganized letters I write him.

"A split personality," he teases me. "The work you send me is faultless. If I can read it. Do you really do it yourself?"

His letters are concise, cut through to the essentials. My letters—I write personal ones the way I talk, tripping over punctuation, my ambition racing ahead of my fingers, my lines full of misprints where I pause to think. We couldn't be more different. He hasn't seemed to mind.

"My secretary can spell," he soothes me when I apologize. "That's not what I need you for." He couldn't be pleasanter to work with.

As I keep saying, I like to work with men; they think differently, they enlarge my horizons. When I am through putting the nuts and bolts together, which I enjoy doing, their suggestions send me back to sources, which I also enjoy. I like to have them in charge, to work up their suggestions, to fit this new material in smoothly, as if it had been there from the beginning. Writing for me is like a jigsaw puzzle, every piece has to dovetail, those nuts and bolts lock together without apparent effort, the finished product flow. I love to work at this. I love to see my colleagues' satisfaction, too, as they recognize my—their—effort.

This man is younger than my sons, but there is no generation gap between us. No gaps of any sort. Back and forth our manila envelopes have gone all year. We know each other's mental characteristics, what we each eat, read, do in our spare time: the women he takes to dinner, the flowers I grow in my garden. I can ask him the most outrageous personal questions—I often do—and he answers without hesitation, or even surprise. And I, who am a very private person, am not embarrassed that he knows intuitively what I conceal from the rest of the world, why I stammer. He is laughing at me now as I look—stare—at him, trying to fit his physical appearance into our friendship. The others are off for the day to see a Mayan temple, leaving us to work uninterrupted, shuffling our papers back and forth.

He picks up my salad plate and stands looking down at me, still laughing.

"Do I pass inspection, Mrs. Fisk?" If he were my age, if I were his, he might have kissed me. It isn't the kiss that matters, it is the current, the trust and pleasure that can flow, rarely and wonderfully, between two people.

At the airport we stand looking at each other again. I memorize the way his hair frames his brow, the fine lines just beginning to etch his generous mouth. I search for and find affection in his eyes. I want to take my courage in my hands, to abandon dignity. I want to say—

"If anything happens to me—those snakes they warn about, the heart condition that frets my doctor—I want you to know that I have loved you." But how can you say that to a man half your age?

"Don't let those head hunters get you," I warn him lightly. "I don't want to lose you."

His hand is equally light on my shoulder. His eyes hold mine. He knows.

"You won't ever lose me," he promises. And is gone.

Day 15

In the false dawn chachalacas call from a distance. I am awakened by a patter of feet overhead where the three new ladies sleep. I moved downstairs when the shifts changed, a mistake, why didn't I leave well enough alone? Upstairs I had bedposts and those windows I kept cracking my head on; fine for drying shirts. Now I have only two nails to hold jeans, my raincoat, my turquoise nightgown. Well, at least I don't have to climb the stairs a dozen times a day to fetch what I have forgotten. My legs have grown lazy this past year.

There comes now a dim murmur of voices above, a toing and froing by flashlight over these stairs, then outside the window. It is really early, black dark, but today we are to move our operations far down the highway before breakfast. Perhaps I misunderstood the hour for Earliest Coffee and Departure? Or didn't listen. Instructions change frequently, I rely on my housemates.

Since I dress faster than they do, and travel lighter, I drift off for a few minutes more sleep, then snap sharply awake. The building is completely silent, I have been left. Swiftly I pull on shirt and jeans. In the dark, again I have had to loan my flashlight. Gathering up sheets and laundry—it is Wash

Day—I run the quarter-mile to the Main House by the light of a small penlight I carry for emergency and have had to use for ten of my days here. The trail is full of obstacles; I can't navigate it by feel.

In Trinidad once, at the Nature Centre, I walked out the long drive late one night, a good half-mile. My flashlight quit. It was dark of the moon, that road runs under trees for most of its length, has steep banks on one side above a ditch, a sharp drop off to a stream on the other. I had walked it for twelve years and would have thought my feet knew every turn and waterhole, but they failed me. I panicked. Only grass growing between the ruts, an occasional puddle, an occasional spatter of stars overhead guided my anxious shuffle. I couldn't tell when I was mid-road or poised on a verge. So now I keep a penlight that I hide from all borrowers, although its beam doesn't extend far, isn't bright enough to pick out a snake on the litter of this path. I wouldn't worry if it weren't that daily I see that scar on Dora's leg. She makes light of it, but after two years she still wears a bandage across her instep. She really means the warnings she gives us.

The Main House is dark and silent as I approach. My pals have left without me? For the first time I look at my watch, and moan. It is only five o'clock! Coffee Hour (and bananas, bread, oranges, peanut butter) would be at six. The residents here are still sleeping, lucky people. Oh well . . . quietly I put kettles on for coffee, slice the last loaf of bread—WHAT?? Did they eat two for dinner last night? Those huge loaves?? Pigs! I make a pillow of my laundry and curl up in a chair. Someone's alarm clock will rouse me in time to set out First Breakfast (and receive surprised thanks; I am usually last to appear). I can nap this afternoon, unless I am baking. I wonder where my housemates went? Off to hunt for pauraques, owls?

The Experienced Crew has the early duty. We leave to dig holes, stretch nets, chop brush, mark location tags; tripping over logs in the forest dimness, giving and receiving orders that are ignored. Then we return to Second Breakfast—potato omelets, biscuits and honey—Diane does us proud. My housemates are serenely at table. They had not gone looking for pauraques and owls at all—just to the biffy and back to their beds.

I make sandwiches for the men who stayed with the nets— each a special order. No butter on Dave's, no marmalade on Trevor's; what can I find but peanut butter for the third? Please? (Nothing.) Helping hands wrap these into confusion, squash oranges and bananas and thermoses on top of them; my loving care is wasted. It looks and feels like rain. Again? I haven't yet eaten. Dora is hinting hopefully about cookies for tonight's dinner. I elect to stay home. Our new habitat looked too open to snare many birds; I won't be needed. Also I seem to be in charge of lunch. How did I become Assistant Cook? Maria, the Mayan, is delighted; she hates to be alone. Why? Is it better not to ask? Between the dogs and her reluctance I am becoming aware that there is more of a security problem on this plantation than we are told. Doubtless related to the refugees from the wars in the west filtering through the forest— homeless, hungry, tough.

I point out to those who question my decision that we are out of bread again—their doing. This second crew are hearty eaters, have demolished six loaves in two days. At $2.00 apiece we can't afford to buy from the neighbor down the road. Besides, she often forgets to bring it. Besides (only modestly I don't mention this), flattery has gone to my head. To my hands. I am turning out cinnamon buns, cheese and bran loaves, whatever variety Diane's shelves afford. Cookies are more of a challenge, as the local cinnamon has little flavor, chocolate chips are priced from $4.50 to $7.00 a package, raisins and nuts are even more prohibitive. I must make do with cocoa and coffee (mocha; a mistake the first time—I reached for the wrong jar, but it proved successful); with sugar sprinkles and grated orange rind. I must also, to my displeasure, make do with our cranky stove. When Diane lights it the process appears onerous, but not too difficult. She sits on the floor, holds the bottom door down with a foot, pushes on a small button with a thumb that seems never to tire (though I'll bet it is well calloused), strikes a half-dozen matches, and presto—well, presto after a bit— the gas flares up from its pipe. Count to about forty, she says cheerfully, rubbing her thumb. Me, I count to three hundred and still can get no flare. Just a nascent callous I resent.

In the late afternoon I stop to chat with young Jaime, hoeing a small vegetable garden. Jaime is the oldest of Maria's eight children. He can clear four net lanes with his sharp machete while we are still struggling with one. His eyes shine as he tells me of his hope to upgrade his position on the plantation, to become Dora's superintendent. He wants to replant her orchards, restore her nursery garden. He is hardworking and wiry; Dora could use three of him. His little garden doesn't appear thrifty to my eyes, but it is neatly edged, and he seems pleased with it. He is puzzled that one of our men has started calling him Jim. I explain that this is a popular name in the States and, after congratulating his industry, go on my way. I scout the mango tree for warblers, make notes on the sex of the redstarts that own territories further along the path—an orange and black male on one, a pugnacious gray and yellow female defending the next. In summer, on breeding territory, they would be paired, but in winter they maintain separate establishments and permit no encroachment.

Jims. From my past they join me as I saunter, welcome companions I conjure up for a lonely hour.

That first Jim: how old would I have been—twelve?—when he so merrily pushed me down the waxed floor of our dancing class? This was held in the parish house of the Unitarian Church, catty-corner across a triangle from my home in Brookline, Massachusetts, at the corner of Warren and Walnut streets. Due to this triangle there were—still are—five houses that consider themselves to be at the corner. From time to time I run into people who claim they lived at this corner I preempt. I have never remembered them, but I remember clearly young Jim and his grabs at my besashed waistline. He loved to polka with me. At the appointed hour we young ladies and reluctant young gentlemen gathered on the parish steps, scuffling our way there through autumn leaves or thumping our galoshes on wooden boardwalks slippery with snow. There were few cars in those days to deliver the pupils of Miss Sears' Tuesday Afternoon Dancing Class, so we walked—although one greatly envied miss used to arrive in a pony cart. The young gentlemen pitched snowballs, the young ladies giggled until we were summoned inside, separated into sexes, to change into the patent leather slippers we carried in bags much like the green felt bookbags we carried later, in Harvard years; maybe the same ones?

We didn't actually dislike Dancing Class, just our teacher, whose task was to drill us in the manners as well as in the steps and holds proper to that distant day. The young ladies, ruffled and bowed, curls primped, waited as girls have always had to wait. The young gentlemen slid across the polished floor, came to roller-skating halts before us, bowed low from the waist, and requested the pleasure of the dance. I loved moving to music, but I was a lanky bean, no doubt awkward, no belle like the beribboned (and simpering, I muttered to my best friend) other young ladies. Never mind. When the polkas came, Jim rushed across the floor as if afraid he might lose me to a dozen eager rivals. With a flourish he grabbed at my waist, placed the required, folded handkerchief midcenter against my back, and, once he had poised me in line, took off with great verve—one, two, three, slide; one, two, three, slide. . . . He was a head shorter than I but made up for this in enthusiasm. I wonder where he is—*if* he is?—these days? The years could not have quenched the leaping of animal spirits that sparked between us. He may have grown portly over the years, as have I, but he would not have become staid. And there would be nothing staid in the answering gleam of my eye if I were to encounter him. Not even being chosen by our sexy pro in my figure skating years later, held tightly in his arms in the finely-timed turns and twists as we danced on the fresh surface of the ice, held the thrill of Jim and his folded handkerchief, his joyous smile. One, two, three, slide . . .

I'd like to see my second Jim again too, although I bet he *would* be staid, with a good golf game, a paunch, a reputation for his martinis. We met at Harvard Summer School—well, you have to do something constructive with your summer at seventeen, I told my parents, who offered no attractive alternatives for me. We sat on the grass in our groups under the elms of Harvard Yard, ate huge peanut butter sandwiches with marmalade for lunch at Billings and Stover for $.15 apiece (I could handle two), studied together. I never dared tell this Lothario that I was a year ahead of him scholastically, a sophisticated Vassar junior to his about-to-be Yale sophomore. At parties I sat at his feet, feeding him sugar lumps. His world was not mine. He came from the glitter and pomp of Newport, where he lived with a wealthy aunt, he went home weekends. His roommate took me out, was vexed that I would not submit to intentions I was too innocent to understand, told lies about me. Jim disappeared, back to his aunt. But by then I had met Brad on the dock of the Weld Boathouse, so except for a short period of puzzlement his disappearance did not matter too much. I remember him, though—do we ever forget our first loves? Stocky, brown-eyed, gentle. He had five names, they rang like bells in my heart. They still can. Never mind that.

What am I doing in this Belizean forest, sheltering under trees half the day from rain? How did I get from feeding sugar lumps to an eighteen-year-old lad to digging in my suitcase in this foreign house for a chocolate bar? No, there is only one left, I must save it for my next transect with Chan, he rarely takes time to eat breakfast. How many countries have I been in since those girlhood days? Living from squalor to luxury, from holey-toed sneakers to golden slippers, from polkas to rejecting a highly placed diplomat in a South American country where Man is King (particularly in a uniform). He wanted me to leave Brad sitting alone while he, in his cups and with lust obvious in his eye, twirled me about the dance floor. There must be some music, some dancing in Belize? I'll have to ask Jaime if he plays an instrument.

Jims. They are strung through my years, a necklace of memories. That Jim in Homestead—a self-taught botanist working for a county too stingy to send him to a conference that would double his value to them. So I did; it didn't cost that much. He couldn't repay me, he couldn't even afford to take his girl to the movies. He used to bring her to me Saturday nights, we would sit out on the steps in the soft Florida air with a beer. In subtropical Florida it rains all summer, weeds grow waist-high. The next fall when I returned from the north on either side of those steps, along the edges of my pond flowered my gardens, weedless. Hours of patient work by thanking hands.

Arizona Jim was a young manager at Muleshoe Ranch, where I did a bird survey for The Nature Conservancy last spring. He treated me as if I also were twenty-eight years old—flattering but not always practical, as when I became stranded on a rock in the middle of a torrent, desperately needing a hand to help me across, too proud to call for it.

Fifth Avenue Jim, who slipped like an eel through the traffic of New York streets, leaving me similarly stranded on a traffic island, surprised that I didn't keep up with him.

"I'm a country girl," I told him, panting, when finally he waited for me. "Three people on the sidewalk is a crowd to me." But he was off again, unheeding.

And then there is that red-headed young Jim at my hardware store, always cheerful, always able to find some small necessity for my living, even if I don't know its name. Happy to heave the big sacks of birdseed I buy.

My book lies face-down on the bed beside me. Why should I read about someone else's life when the pages of my own ripple their happinesses around me?

There was another Jim. I've turned that page quickly, on purpose. We all have our failures. He had green eyes. I loved him.

Still Day 15

Before dinner a car rattles up to the gate, and a stocky man with disordered gray hair, a wholly unexpected visitor, descends. He is a treasured friend, I am overjoyed to see him. Unfortunately he is here only briefly, on professional business. His eyes seek me out at the dinner table, that familiar smile tugs at the corner of his mouth, but we have no chance really to talk. He brings mail and, after dinner, fishing in his briefcase, hands me a letter.

I slit it open and the world of those people I love back home crumbles. All those bricks painfully laid up over recent years, built into walls to keep them, me, safe, collapse in dust. It is nothing I can talk about, nothing of my doing. The road taken years ago by someone else has come to its predictable end, the last pieces of a jigsaw puzzle I have worked on for ten years have fallen into place. Some griefs are unendurable. I sit in my usual corner, a book on my lap. Mark's eyes rest on me thoughtfully. We have been friends for years, traveled together in difficult circumstances, although it is his wife with whom I carry on our correspondence.

When his conference ends he walks me outside, to a bench in the obscurity of trees.

"Please," I ask him, "just for a moment, Mark. Please put your arm around me?" I throw my head back, proud in the dim light. "I am not leaning on you, Mark, you know I stand on my own feet. But just for a moment . . ."

His arms come strong about me, hold me until I stop shaking. He asks no questions, just is there, solid, comforting, his breath warm in my hair. Finally I lift my head, my lips brushing his cheek in thanks. We sit on the bench, I tell him. He listens without comment—the kindest gift of friendship. I am dry-eyed, factual. He comments on this.

"You don't cry."

"No!" I hear a bitterness in my voice I rarely allow. "I used to cry as a child. Probably it annoyed my siblings, got me what I wanted from my parents. But when Brad died . . . *what good does crying do?*"

I walk back and forth, making a path in the dewy grass, my head thrown back again. Not in pride, but to contemplate the stars of a sky that is half a continent away from the obscuring lights of cities, the evil that can lurk in cities. In memory I hear myself sobbing the last time I permitted myself this luxury. Spread out on a bed, hammering with my fists, moaning like—like a dog.

"How clear—how distant are those stars. Other worlds, indifferent to our affairs." To a dog, moaning in anguish.

"Nothing has ever really mattered to me since then. Whatever comes is like wind blowing by me, like surf that runs up to my feet, then pulls back, sibilant. I hear sounds but they don't reach me. I see the stars, they are cold. But I can't deny my children. It's my blood they carry in them. And Brad's."

A lone planet reflects in the surface of the pond, a distant diamond.

"They may not like you, you may not always like them, but they are yours, you spawned them. You aren't just a sponsor"—I hear the bitterness again—"although you are supposed to act like one. They grow up to be people. Your relationships ebb and flow. They lay their babies in your arms, and these grow up to be people too, and these also are yours. Below whatever surface levels of caring or not caring, approval or disapproval, pain or happiness flows a current until the day you die. Or they do, first. For as long as either of you remembers the other. Love—obligation—the name doesn't affect it. It runs at different speeds over time, turned or delayed by circumstances. You can't ignore its strength even when you want to. It is beyond your control; it is what determines you as a person.

"If a child of mine—of Brad's—comes to me, he comes also from my father, and Brad's—very different breeds of men; and from their wives. From old J. C.; from Fanny Maleska, that Vermont woman named for an Indian chief. From a minister who lies under a stone in Hyde Park, whose farm now lies under the city hall of Brooklyn; from that lean westerner in museum photographs who guided covered wagons over the Oregon Trail."

All of whom loved, and bred, and as surely also paced in grass under stars. Their blood runs in the smallest of my grandchildren, gurgling in his mother's backpack. They lay on me a duty I have to fulfill.

I sigh, study again the remoteness of those stars. Mark does not move. A current runs between us, too. I search again for words.

"When I am discouraged—who isn't?—when I decide that I have done everything I need to do in life, that I can now let go if I wish, with honor. . . . My years have brought me to where I can no longer function as I want to. When I wonder why I don't just quit, make room for someone else, why do I keep on? One of these young people, or their parents—parents need help too—or a girl one was in love with last year, a boy one is living with this year, the ramifications expand endlessly—one of them appears on my doorstep, needing help. And I can't quit." I sigh again. "Maybe that's what grandparents are for?"

From far back in my past, at the edge of memory, I am aware of a dark skirt rustling; a grandmother I knew only briefly has her arms around me. She wears boned lace high about her throat, my fingers pull at it. Her arms comfort me in some small child's small crisis. The wind that has blown over her grave these many years will blow over mine; the blood goes on. There will always be a child in need of comfort.

"And maybe that's what grandchildren are for?" I query

Mark wryly. "To keep us going, head into the wind?"

I am sitting now, his hand twined firmly in mine.

"You've been through worse," he tells me, knowing. "I'll be back in the States in a few days, I'll see what I can do . . ." He moves in the big world, knows means I have no access to of handling problems. He is competent.

Now it is his lips that brush my cheek. He tips my face up to his when we rise, kisses me gently. "Sarah and I don't have children. Perhaps we can borrow one of yours?" He teases from me the ghost of a laugh.

"Take your choice," I offer him. The strength that flows from his embrace will let me sleep this night.

Friendship. Willingness to help someone in trouble. Love for your fellow man. The protection men have given me. You can't count on it, you can't demand it. You never know where— or if—it will surface. But *in extremis,* if you leave yourself open, if you ask for nothing. . . . Well, I did ask. Don't be so damned proud you don't ask. If it is someone like Mark. . . . There aren't many like him, I've been lucky.

Surprisingly, I do sleep. Early next morning I see the transect crew slipping by my window. I dress and run after them. Later I go with the others to the forest, slip and slide in mud, at noon bring cuddled in my hand the black and white and red-gartered manakin with scarlet head and yellow pantaloons, its cold white eye disdaining us, that none of us had expected to see. But I keep away from the river flowing green-gray and swift between its banks, carrying around its bends whatever flotsam has fallen or dropped—or jumped—into its current overnight. Friendship also carries obligations.

Day 16. *Midmorning*

It is so humid that sweat runs down my nose. I have had to punch down my bread dough a second time. I had planned a hike to search a far corner of the property where I might find a species we have not yet listed, but it is too hot. Diane's typewriter is balking again, and I am not a mechanic. Forgetting this last fact, I decide to restring a deck chair in need of attention. Heaven knows how a roll of green plastic strips found its way to this country, but there it is, on Diane's shelf. We need chairs. I will earn my keep, energize that breakfast I ate too much of, surprise everyone with my industry. I didn't mind a bit when they all vanished into fog, jammed uncomfortably into the overloaded conveyances, leaving the verandah empty and peaceful.

I hunt up tools and set to work. The dogs supervise with a curiosity that soon fades. It is too hot, and obviously I am going to be scrumbling about on my knees for some time. Orioles talk in the powderpuff bush below us. A half-hour later, as always when I get myself into any carpentry or handwork, I am swearing, muttering that if God had wanted me to be a handyman He would have given me a different kind of brain, put other genes in my makeup.

I have managed to take the chair apart. I haven't yet lost the screws and washers (but I will, I will). I put them above the reach of a dog's languid tail. There is no wind to remove them, just my own clumsy movements. Then I find the task goes more easily than I had expected. I shake the sweat from my nose and sit back in false pride. False because immediately the plastic curls back in knots like a telephone cord, like the Virginia creeper tendrils that used to snarl my nets in Florida. Oh, well—I dealt with those, and I am in no hurry, I can handle this stuff. I remember my bread dough and deal with it, which eases a crick growing in my back.

Some animal must be prowling nearby, the dogs set up a terrible row, pound along the verandah, down the stairs. I grab for the screws. A four-legged animal, or a two? I see nothing, no one, but their barking is horrendous. Maria has left, I am alone. This plantation is vulnerable, but I wouldn't want to be an intruder sustaining a charge by those Dobermans, who now return, inspect my accomplishment as far as it has gone, and settle down again. Our Ladies' Quarters are beyond the compound fence, but since my housemates always go off clanking with their cameras and binoculars, only their clothing could be stolen. My own camera is where? I don't use it often; not often enough, I learn when I get home and need photographs for programs. At this distance programs haven't seemed important, or even probable, so I neglect to carry it about with me.

I think of those northern activities—the world of meetings, concerts, lectures to organize or attend, a red light flickering on my telephone secretary, friends stopping in for breakfast or lunch. (Well, a cheese sandwich and a hard winter tomato is lunch, isn't it? Of a sort?) Newspapers to be riffled through, then tied to take to the dump. TV telling what someone thinks will happen politically if something else happens—if, always if. Trucks and cars, a yellow school bus letting off children. The winter streets of our small town empty of tourist traffic. What a blessing, to jaywalk anywhere! A plane, too high to hear, trailing its silver trail from London over our salt pond, ducks trailing their triangles across the water. A busy world of people.

Well, there are people here. Why am I suddenly uneasy, forlorn? Is it because I see myself growing old, have settled for a morning on a sunny verandah instead of working in the field? Other people grow old too, get deaf and creaky, have to change their living style. Stop whining, Fisk. It's how you adjust to change that matters. Count your blessings. So I do, but I don't enjoy the need to do so.

While I was whining I was not paying attention to what I was doing. Pulling the last green strip tight, I see that I have made a mistake. I undo my braiding, straighten the strip, wind again, fasten the last screw in place with pliers, massage my knees. Now what? The day is only half over. Lunch. Peanut butter? It is too hot for peanut butter, but it is too hot to explore all those packages of leftovers in the fridge, too. Cheese. A hunk of this is right in front, as I open the door. Should I wait until I have gone through that onerous process of lighting the stove, wait until my bread bakes and then have cheese on a hot crust? What is wrong with having cheese on a cracker now, and more on a hot crust an hour from now? Nothing, nothing at all. Whose life is this? Who cares about my figure? I hunt for a book to read.

I needn't tell my friends at home about this exciting, adventurous life I lead in foreign countries. I stretch out, comfortable in my refurbished chair.

Day 17

June has come running to the banding table, excited, with, she says, a Great antshrike in a bag. We are working on Hummingbird Highway some thirty miles from home, limping back and forth in the cars. Although the Highway is the main road from Belmopan south, I don't suppose a dozen cars or trucks have gone by the concealed clearing where we are sitting about on rotting logs. This is hardwood forest that has been selectively lumbered. Saplings left to grow are now magnificent trees, although our section must have been hit by hurricanes, for it is thick with the dark green fountains of the cahune palms that come in after blowdowns. The second growth is too tangled to push through; when we get restless we must walk out on the road. Up hill is a farm set about with fruit trees and flowers, the farmer's wife looks at us and our telescopes with curiosity. Down hill is a quarry. Trails lead off in twisting paths to huts. We bird and botanize, stick our noses into roadside flowers, have returned to find June all atwit with her catch. She is reluctant to put her hand into its bag and extract it; for good reason, a shrike's bill is built for tearing flesh. I volunteer. I handled our native shrikes in Florida, they weren't as bad as their reputation. They are smaller than the tropical species, their bills are smaller. In Trinidad I took Great ones—flamboyant beauties, the male black and white, the female chestnut. Both have a heavy, hooked bill. As with cardinals and grosbeaks, you must learn to hold their heads tilted at an angle. Cooperation isn't readily forthcoming. To hold one for photographs is a different matter. At home I have a first-class one—well, I think it first class—of the first one I ever netted, in Trinidad. I was collecting weights and measurements for Richard ffrench's *Guide*. Innocently I had held my prize—a male—up into a patch of sunlight in one hand, adjusting camera and focus with the other. It was a standoff. I got the photograph, the shrike got a three-cornered hunk of flesh from the soft base of my thumb. Blood streams down my wrist—the picture makes a hit on all my programs. My files hold no photo of the female, which I caught later. I had learned my lesson.

So today I tell my eager friends that if they will come out into the sun, will focus while I hold this bird enclosed in my fist, I will drop my fingers long enough for them to take one quick shot. No pretty posing, no second chance. If anyone wishes a more artistic presentation I will hand over our subject. No volunteers. And, of course, hearty laughter as the bird poses with head bent, my thumb firmly and painfully anchored in its bill. I have lots of photographs of birds chewing on that thumb. Schoolchildren, sadists at heart, love them. Then Henry asks me for a closeup of that notched bill. My friend, Henry! I oblige. If you are in a position to do a favor for someone you do it, I was taught. Love makes the world—and Kodak—go round.

Day 18

Spending that fine sunny day at Hummingbird Highway was a fine idea and a lot of fun, but WHEN will I learn? The roadside we walked foamed with a vine—a weed surely, it was everywhere, overrunning shrubs and trees: beautiful but not fragrant. I put my nose in it to see, picked a bouquet of it for the Common Room. There were other flowers, scattered sparsely, we sniffed these too. When will I learn?

I have many childhood memories of lying in bed in the spring stirring honey into shimmering bubbles in a wine glass with a small silver spoon, licking this to alleviate an inflamed throat. Allergies were a field then just being discovered. Our doctor was a pioneer studying pollens, experimenting on me for cures. So far—and every spring I am still afflicted—no one has found a better rememdy than that honey, preferably now laced with rum. In Buffalo my problem was elm trees, it was an elm city. The trees of Paris I didn't analyze, but springtime in Paris I don't wish to experience again. The famous chestnut trees bloomed below our hotel balcony at the Rond Point. I used to stagger out, wrapped in a scarlet coat over my night-gown, to watch the parades for visiting Heads of State. At my appearance armed guards on every roof around sprang to attention, rifles at the ready. If you planned to shoot a Head of State, would you wrap yourself in scarlet? Nor do I want to see spring in Zagreb, where one Easter Sunday I lay miserable and voiceless in bed, listening to the church bells that rang all day. My only amusement, except for a terrified young waiter who scuttled in and out with trays. I don't know why he was terrified. I was respectably covered; I had neither the strength nor the inclination to chase him. Because I couldn't talk? Certainly not in Croatian! He brought me plum brandy for breakfast, a custom I wish we had in this country. I'll ask Diane if the liquor store in Belmopan carries it, it would burn my vocal cords open.

The year I went to Mexico to see if I could handle travel without Brad, handle myself, I returned speechless, running a temperature of 102°F. My gentle allergist found me limp on her steps the next morning.

"But I haven't been treating you for tropical trees!" she cried in dismay. "You didn't tell me you were going to Mexico!"

She was sympathetic to my grief, letting me sleep out my exhaustion on her treatment table. She saw me not as a patient to be needled and dispatched but as someone desperately in need of kindness. Many a time since when someone has come to me taking up time I am reluctant to spare, I remember this generous woman. Years later, visiting in Washington, I carried a pot of spring tulips to her office. Her name was no longer on the door, and I could not find her in the telephone book.

Today I am reading and sleeping on my bed here in the pines where my throat is more comfortable. The others went birding in a swamp (which they later report to have been full of herons and shorebirds. I saw plenty of herons and shorebirds those years in the Everglades.). I am to make cinnamon rolls against their return, but my personal intake is still rum and honey—a diet that carries me comfortably and drowsily through the day.

At noon I am over at the Main House, halfheartedly exploring the fridge, when Steve appears, decides also against its contents. Like me he is half-ill, and weary.

"You are lucky," he says. He is a professional, here on a quasi-vacation, getting experience that will lead to a better job. My eyes question him. At the moment I am not feeling lucky, just old, and ill.

"You don't have to work." He isn't being catty, just wistful.

I agree. "Only I think *you* are lucky, Steve. When you wake up in the morning you have to go to work, to support your children, in order to eat. You have work to go to, your day always has to have accomplishment in it. At my age you have nothing really to get up for, you have to hunt for ways to justify your existence. They aren't easy to find. Too often when I go to bed at night I ask myself, And what did you accomplish today, do for someone else? If I can write a check that's for someone else's involvement, it doesn't put me personally into the scene, it's not the same. I don't want to subsidize professional work, I want to do it myself. I'm reaching the point where young people look at me and say, NO, we can't ask her, she's too old to take with us. That's rough. I want to contribute. I don't know the answer to this."

Steve doesn't either. "You make good bread," he comforts me, lamely. "You are good at training people, and extracting hummingbirds." He knows this isn't enough, reaches over to pat my hand, holds it. We sit in a silence of friendship.

"Having friends is an accomplishment," he says, reading my thoughts.

I smile at him. "You are right. I *am* lucky."

Day 19

I am still coddling my throat. I sit on the verandah, making study skins of a dusky red tanager with a vermilion crown patch, of a Clay-colored robin whose name describes him perfectly, and of a plump little wren vigorously spotted on breast and tail. This last will not turn out well; it is a small bird, my fingers are too big. I consider this occupation as useful to our program as my running around in the forest. Certainly it is less competitive. I was given no envious looks when the group departed after breakfast.

A study skin is made by slitting the belly of a freshly dead bird with a scalpel, hoping it will not prove so greasy with fat that the delicate integument will tear before I can get even one leg cleaned. I disembowel my subject, turn it inside out, remove the body, the brain, the eyes, the tongue, leaving as little flesh as possible to attract insects. Turn it right side out again. With care. Wash it, dry and fluff its feathers, stuff it with cotton. Twitch its shoulders, straighten its head, spread its tail, and bake it overnight in a slow oven, again to defeat those pesky insects. For the purpose of—how did you guess?—its being studied by those not fortunate to handle the bird live, where it lives.

If it is the breeding season, if male and female are similar, I sex them by exploring their innards. (There are scientific words for this.) If the sexes differ in color—dimorphic is the word—I need only to glance at their plumage. Some tropical females are so different from the males that you think you hold another species in your hand, which is confusing until you learn. Wing and tail lengths can differ with sex, too. You try to determine age by the colors and condition of the plumage. There is a lot to know about birds. I should know more.

Each species is different. Some are so tough-skinned I may work quickly and successfully, some thin-skinned, so that sooner or later my patient labor goes for nothing. Some have almost no flesh on their wing bones, some so much that I must make a slit between these, pick, pluck, then sew the slit up again. Tedious work, with fingernails often more helpful than the tools I carry in a battered shaving kit—gift of an admirer apprehensive about my sharp scalpels and forceps. I am not very good at this. June is excellent but claims she didn't come to Belize to indulge in such a demanding pastime. I can take a bird apart all right, but stuffing it back together so it will fool you is another matter. Lying on a tray in a museum it isn't going to fool anybody, anyway. I am willing, and I have the time. And while I work I can sit on this fine airy verandah, the dogs at my feet, clouds parading across the sky, orioles talking to each other in the blossoms below me, binoculars at hand. Who could ask for a better way to spend a morning?

The tanager and the wren were road kills. We get few down here, cars are too old, roads too rough for speeding. In Florida, where highways are ruler straight and speed limits ignored, road kills were common. I would stop, back up to look at a bird or a snake I had passed to judge its condition, wait while a truck—or several—thundered by, often crushing my specimen; run into the road before another came at me. I retrieved some good birds for the University this way. One morning I counted twenty-seven dead or injured gallinules (moorhen is the new name) on the speedway to Florida Power & Light Co. Moorhens are chicken-sized birds, slow-moving as they cross the roads from canal to canal. I tossed the dead off under the casuarinas (those are trees, darkly lining that road). The injured I put out of their misery and tossed. A few that seemed only dazed I removed to safety. One appeared in such good shape that I set it on the floor of my car to recuperate, if it did not die of internal injuries. When I returned from my appointment it was exploring the car with interest. I opened the door and it took off. In leisurely fashion, which was probably its death on another day.

The wren in my hand had tangled itself in the net in the manner of wrens and had become strangled. Which is why we run our nets often, so they won't. Accidents are a risk you must accept if you work with any animal, including man. In order to learn, to further survival. You can't learn without study. You can't study without handling. You can't handle without somewhere along the line a mishap. Ask your M.D. Of course it distresses you. I am careful with this wren. Too late.

Interest in birds has zoomed in the last few years as we have become aware of their role and their value as monitors of our changing world environments. It is hard to believe that when I went to classes at the Buffalo Museum of Science our biologist could go out with permit and gun to collect fifty and more birds a day. He told us how he would sit up at night in his station wagon to skin them out. By feel. His fingers must have been far more dextrous than mine! There his specimens would be, laid out in neat rows a few days later for us to examine.

There they still are, in cases, valuable. When our country passed protective laws collectors moved to other more lenient countries. Now they too, seeing their wildlife declining in its competion with human life, are passing laws. Enforcement is spotty, though, and untrained. And the price of wildlife for sale, for pets and pelts, becomes higher and more remunerative each year.

Our museums must now depend on road and window kills, on loons and gulls and sea and shorebirds picked up dead on beaches—if people know enough to deliver them frozen to universities or nature centers for specimens, to laboratories in the case of seabird or pesticide kills, for pathological examination to determine causes of death. Oil ingestion, mercury, red tide? Aspergillosis or other diseases? Which chemicals? As the importance of such studies becomes more and more apparent, rehabilitation centers are springing up all over the country. I am supposed to be at my desk at home right now, making a survey of the success some of these centers have with their released birds. If they band them, which only the more scientific-minded do. I am supposed to be finding out about that, too. This is a sedentary job, suitable to my age, but I'm not very sedentary, so I haven't started it yet. Next year . . .

The good specimens I make must go to educational centers. The not-so-good I use in my own educational talks, pointing out how thick and water-resistant the feathers are, the variety of foot and bill shapes and uses. My failures, the edible parts and birds too badly damaged, go to feed hawks and owls at rehabilitation centers. Natural food. Nature's recycling. All of these must be reported on forms to the government.

In Florida neighborhood children hiking or biking to school would bring me birds they picked up along the roadsides—usually mourning doves, which are slow to move out of the way of cars. Being broke at the time, I supplemented my diet with these, until I became aware of the amount and potential of the agricultural sprays used in local fields where the birds fed. The children and I would examine their gifts, discuss what might have killed them, put in my aviary those only damaged, study plumages. If this made them late for school, as The Bird Lady I had become a sort of adjunct teacher. I talked to their assemblies. Classes of younger ones would march singing up my lane with their picnic lunches, often bringing mice for my hawks and owls. I was summoned to the school-yard to catch injured or strange birds. The most notable of these was "a baby peacock," a report that brought me flying, butterfly net at the ready, to capture a Purple gallinule (moorhen), a bird of the Everglades as confused as I to find itself on a barren athletic field.

What skill I have in skinning birds was learned at the University of Miami, the nearest I ever came to any academic training in ornithology. I didn't want to take time from field work for book study. (I wasn't going to live that long. That was twenty years ago; I am a poor prognosticator.) Bud Owre (Dr. Oscar T.) could skin out a bird in minutes, making only the tiniest slit. Mine go from breastbone to vent. His Cuban refugee sculptor assistant could take a hopeless specimen of mine, tweak its feathers, realign its shoulders, and presto—there would be a bird, practically alive. Working with experts breeds humility as well as friendship. Wilfredo's ambition was to skin an elephant. I could use Wilfredo here today, I think, gathering up my tools. After I left Florida, whenever I went through Miami I would visit the Bird Range, talk with the new crop of students, hunt through the drawers with great pride to find specimens I had contributed (which Wilfredo obviously must have redone), neatly labeled, all data correctly entered. From Cape Cod, summers, I would send Bud northern birds he would not get in Miami, with cards reading "Happy Memories."

Once—I keep telling you that bird banding has fringe benefits, is full of delights—I underwent a marriage proposal while skinning out a pile of house sparrows. I was working in my Florida chickee (that's a sort of thatched summerhouse—the Cherokee Indians live in them, they had built me one by my pond). I was comfortable in its shade, feathers and bodies scattered about my table, red-winged blackbirds splattering in the reeds. A widowed photographer drove up in a house trailer. He insisted I inspect it. He wished to marry, he stated. His specifications were a woman who knew about birds (he could see half a dozen of my nets from where we sat); who could write (I had just had a paper published in an ornithological journal); who would be willing to drive about the United States and Alaska, camping for weeks at a time in refuges. A fine life, I thought regretfully, in the right company. He would take care of the photography. He was not a fussy eater.

He didn't seem to notice my occupation, my messy fingers and scalpels. He didn't seem to care about *me,* whether *I* was a fussy eater. He discussed finances. I kept my eyes demurely lowered, finishing one sparrow, starting another. He discussed sex, which flummoxed me. When I don't know how to handle a situation I freeze (become frigid might be the better phrase here). My concentration on my birds became extreme. I said nothing, not wishing to hurt his feelings. Actually I was speechless trying to control hilarity, trying to be polite. At one point I offered him a beer, out of manners. He turned out to be a teetotaler. How could I have arranged for my evening rum in his van? I'm afraid I disappointed him; he left abruptly.

The sparrows turned out not badly. Bud Owre whooped and hollered when I told him why.

Day 20

Where am I? Flipping through these disorderly scribbled notes, I see that I might well call this journal, if it becomes a journal, if it reaches the need of a title, The Men in My Life. Brad was the only one I really loved, but a woman does notice the men who walk in and out of her front door. The women too—I kept my eye on these latter. I didn't permit poaching.

Two of these men, both journalists, go back to my twenties. Ardis was a small, friendly man, grateful in the Depression for a job on the local paper. Julie, his wife, did free-lance work. We liked each other; they were both trying to persuade me that I could, should write. They were streetwise, outside our social circle: I can't remember how I met them. Maybe at our Little Theatre the winter my Boston accent had placed me in a Galsworthy play. All I remember about THAT was that I had to take my stockings off. On stage! Shocking, for that time. The man, the lead whose job was to balance me as I performed this, *was* in our social circle, given to surreptitious caresses if he could trap me backstage. Ardis was amused by my Puritan indignation, taught me a couple of useful tricks I've been grateful for over the years. He got me a job writing book reviews. They must have been terrible, what did I know then? (What do I know now, for that matter?) He tried to pull me into their field, but I was happy in my domesticity. He opened windows for me, though, and bought me an occasional beer in speakeasies until gossip reached my in-laws. A proper young matron in those days didn't, shouldn't, anyhow, drink beer in midafternoon with a married man. Not in my family's mores. Brad was distressed; I had to stop. Or did Ardis and Julie just move away? I don't remember. I was a women's-righter even then, stubborn, and pretty fascinated, not by the swinging doors that led to beer but by the glimpses of his newspaper world.

The second journalist was sent to us during the Depression, jobless and hungry. A redheaded lad, he became my gay younger brother. (I am old enough to use "gay" in its original, centuries-old context of merry, of constant laughter, of days alive with someone to play with. Not all language changes are for the better.) Crosby helped me train our boys. They were what— four, five? A strenuous age indoors in winter. He frolicked on the floor with them, mended their toys, invented games, helped me stuff spinach and custard into their mouths. Brad would arrive home from work, we would laugh our way through dinner. And I was equally useful to Crosby. He took a job handling publicity for the Little Theatre, where "older women"— they must have been in their thirties—found him attractive and merry. He needed protection.

Like all good things, this era came to an end—I think the midnight we drove one of his lady admirers home to find her husband pacing their walk with a gun (he was dramatic too). Meg went back to teaching costume design afternoons, instead of setting a stage by her fireside with candles, wine, a single rose—and a furious look at me when, the picture of innocence, I also arrived for tea. (Well, it was my car Crosby needed to get there, why shouldn't I come along?) Crosby left for a better job in New York, I became pregnant again and returned to the diaper routine. Years later I asked a friend to riffle through the New York telephone books and see if he could trace my former playmate. A note came back: "No, but here is a picture of his racing car." Then that friend too disappeared, leaving me with a permanent mystery.

Matt. It's Matt I want to tell you about. I had another Colonel besides the one here on this list of men whose interest in my work, whose friendship, picked me up at different times of need, sent me exploring down paths I would never have found for myself, who have led me to the crossroad I now stand at. In his quiet way Matt was responsible for those published papers that occupy little room on my shelf but are a source of keen satisfaction to me and even, occasionally, are used as references in the august publications of professionals. Matt didn't know much about birds, but as head of training in a sensitive government agency he surely knew how to handle and to motivate people. I used to stop off with him spring and fall on my migrations, vent my pent-up energy running on his beach, do my laundry, wash my waist-length hair, brush it dry on his deck in view of his curious neighbors. I trapped the abundant house sparrows at his bird feeder for him, buried them for fertilizer around a small pine he had planted in his sand dune yard. I was a different breed than the widows always after him. No cocktail charmer, no bridge partner in pearls and high heels I. I would cook our dinners, line up casseroles in his freezer so he would remember me, and go on my way for another six months.

I've forgotten how we met. At a cocktail party? He showed up at a U. S. Fish & Wildlife banding station in Maryland where I worked before I set up on my own in Florida, where I learned my trade under Gladys Cole, whose graduates are now scattered all over the States; where Chan used to come over weekends to work with us and teach us. Those weekends were wild—a dozen of us might sleep in a motel cottage on couches, on the floors. I would be up at 4:30 A. M. helping Gladys get breakfast, make sandwiches. It would be 8:00 P. M. before we were back, dinner still to cook, the day's catch to verify, dishes to wash. But during the week there were only Gladys and I in a lonely area on the edge of an unsavory town, in a marsh, scrubby woods full of poison ivy. Gladys was always frightened. Matt took to stopping by to make sure we were safe. Interested as well as gallant, he sometimes stayed on to help, sometimes brought his house guests to be instructed in wildlife research—once an extraordinarily pretty blonde. "Of course I have a pretty secretary," he replied crisply when I teased him. "Why else does a man make his way to the top?" Over time she and I too became friends, and then her navy husband. Bird banding has its benefits . . .

Certainly Matt was one. If I trained him to help me with recording, he never trained me to accept his tobacco chewing. One winter he wrote me from Tobago, asking me to come help Eleanor Alefounder set up her estate there as a sanctuary, as Don Eckelberry and I (and a score of better-heeled birders) had done at Asa Wright's Spring Hill Estate on Trinidad. Knowing I would be flying down for a Trustee's Meeting at Asa's he advertised Tobago's swimming and bird life at Pigeon Point, the snorkeling on Bucco Reef, his skill at building sundowners. And Eleanor, whom promptly I loved, returning to her big house for eight years. Of course I went. I taught Matt to take wood creepers and tanagers (and all their feathers, please) out of nets for me. I noted data for Richard ffrench's *Guide*, then being written. I brought the head of National Audubon, his Research Department, and all the birders I could gather up, all of whom knew more about sanctuaries than I did, to have tea on her gallery. Chachalacas flew up on their laps, spilling their tea. Chachalacas are the size of a hen, the national bird of Tobago. You don't just brush them off your knee, however startled both of you are. Motmots perched on the railings, woodpeckers supped at sugar water, thrush ran about the kitchen counters where I squeezed pitchers of orange juice. It was glorious.

My friendship with Matt built mostly by letter and the few days I would stop on my migrations. Trained by my father, and with the feminine desire to please, I would fit myself with amusement into his dictatorial schedule of beach walking and TV mysteries, disrupt his social life with the local ladies. What he liked to do, what he could do, was to draw out the best in people, uncover talents we weren't aware of, turn amateurs into professionals. He made us believe in ourselves.

"I can't do it!" I remember wailing at him one night. "I don't know *how*. *Why* do I keep trying to do what I've no training for? Why don't I just stick to making cookies and sewing on buttons?"

He had looked down on me. I was sitting on the floor by his fire, drying my hair, leafing through his scrapbooks, my own work pushed irritably aside.

"You can do anything you want to," he had said quietly.

I couldn't look away from his stern blue eyes.

"What's the trouble?"

I swallowed. "Brad said that to me too, not long before he died." I hesitated. "I have always wondered if he knew he was on borrowed time those last months. He kept trying to build up my confidence: I've never had much. But if you and he both think . . ." My voice trailed off. I swallowed again. Matt's eyes still held mine, but I was looking through them to a life long past.

"Yes," he said, again quietly, and returned to his reading. I can still hear his voice, smell his cigar. They have buoyed me many a time when projects I take on become too difficult for me. My staircase on Cape Cod has a rogues' gallery of men who have had real influence on my life. Often as I pass I put out my hand to Matt's small photograph.

"Thanks, my friend" I say. "I'm sorry you aren't here to see what you pushed me into doing."

Going and coming I would weed his garden patch for him, write him when he was in the hospital what was blooming, what birds used the birdbath he had planted with ivy one day when I was there, how the skimmers flew at sunset low along his beach. As you see, I loved him, although we passed only the customary undemonstrative social pecks of greeting and farewell. Like the other men I have worked with.

"Love in the open hand," Vincent Millay once wrote in a sonnet. . . . As one should bring you cowslips in a hat swung from the hand, or apples in her skirt." You don't need your hand held, a kiss at the doorstep, when you have that. I like to be kissed, though. It's just the wrong men who do it.

During Matt's last illness I traveled far to see him. He would not have me admitted. Pride? Did he want me to remember him lean, with that cleft Irish chin, shaggy brows, blue eyes laughing at me as on one day when I flared in his garden—

"Give me your hand! All this time I've known you and I've never even held it!"

He had shifted his hoe, let me study a hand that had wrestled barbed wire and cattle and camp ropes; had held guns, the indoor trappings of high office, thousands of bourbons. Grown soft now with age, deeply lined. I wanted to lift it to my cheek, but I was too shy. He must have known. Under my layers of veneer I am emotionally eight years old, and it shows. Why do we go through life pretending, covering over? Why can't we tell people we love them?

Why am I remembering all this, a world away in Belize? What does it have to do with bird banding? With my walking? For I have been walking hard and fast for half an hour now. I must be miles from the compound, trying to work this—what? the memories, the pain I try to keep buried, locked in the boxes of my subconscious?—out of my system. I've come to an old road that parallels the highway. I tried to take a shortcut home but it ended in a dump, in woods I couldn't break through. I'm having to retrace my steps. It's dark, I have no flashlight, I'll be late for supper. Why have I let the past flood over me so abruptly, so painfully? What brought this on? Do you carry those you have loved always with you? Even after they are gone? Even when it was so long ago?

Yes.

Stumbling along the broken pavement I can't let go. Here I am, I rail at myself, come to Belize to do research, instead scribbling in a notebook. I wrote a book, surprisingly, accidentally, a couple of years ago—a late blooming at my age for sure. So, because old ladies haven't that much to do to keep them out of mischief (you can't dig in a Cape Cod garden in winter; my pineland is too acid and full of roots and rabbits for a garden anyway), I have started rather vaguely writing in the pages of my bird diary down here. As always I don't know what I am doing, or how to go about it. A book has to have a title, a beginning, and an end. I've done that, I know that. Only not what should go in the middle. My editor tried tentatively to suggest, but he thinks differently, his vocabulary

confuses me. Besides, he knows me only from the careful letters I write him, trying to make a good impression. He doesn't
know the real me. He doesn't see me bumbling about in my
various half-baked activities. He doesn't see me here, stumbling in the dark, besieged and ragged with loss.

I don't know the real me either. You all can tell me who I
am if ever these sheets see the light of day. If I trip once more
on this darned road they won't even see tomorrow.

I *must* be near our turnoff, it's somewhere near here, I can't
find it in the dark. It's opposite a tall pine that arches at its
top, out in a field. Only it's too dark to see out in the field.
That pinpoint of light down through the bushes—would that
be the candle in the shower room? Someone home?

Anyway, go back. Go back to where I am sitting on the
floor by Matt's fire. He is smoking one of his smuggled Cuban
cigars while he reads and I flip through his scrapbooks. Go
back to where I am sitting on the edge of Brad's chair in
Washington, rubbing my thumb down his beloved shoulder,
my cheek against his ear. They are both dead.

Often I wish I were.

Day 21

Today we pack picnic baskets, fill all the thermoses, take lots of fruit—it will be HOT. This is to be a Culture Day, with some birdwatching along the route thrown in. It will be a long drive to Xunantunich, a Mayan temple, the highest building in the country, but Dora feels we should see more of her country. So I am balanced on one hip in the front seat, trying to keep disentangled from the gear shift, listening to a lecture on the formation of the limestone hills that rise and fall along the road like illustrations from a child's fairy tale. Dora has names for them. If you think the Papago Indian names I tried to pronounce in Arizona were difficult, you should try curling your tongue about the Mayan language! The sharp line that used to show the demarcation between the Miocene beach and the limestone of the hardwood forest was destroyed by Hurricane Hattie in the sixties. Dora promises to show us Hattieville, a shack town where the people of the city were moved inland to escape the surges of the waves that swept over and through the coastal mangroves, drowning the land for fifteen miles inland.

We stop here and there to photograph, to set up telescopes, glad to get out and stretch. Finally we come to a broad river, the Mopan. It is Sunday, family groups are picnicking on its banks. Little girls run about in starched dresses, little boys jiggle fish poles. We cross the water on a raft, one car at a time, loaded carefully. We also are loaded carefully according to our weights.

The temple grounds, also with family groups eating, are a National Reserve. There is a simple open shelter, a topographic map on a table, a uniformed guard who knows Dora. The temple itself—there is only one—is also small, a diminutive echo of the great buildings at Tikal, not too far distant across the Guatemalan border. As only Dora and I know the glory of Tikal, no one is disappointed; on the contrary, they are enchanted. We cluster about the water fountain, photograph, bird hunt, then the guard groups us with his other visitors for instruction.

Xunantunich was the ceremonial center of a civilization, a major city dating far back into B.C., long antedating Tikal. Thousands of homes were built around its satellite area, now lost in jungle. Three sites not yet excavated are larger than Guatemala's showpiece of Tikal with its great temples, its now visible history. These Mayan mounds dot the country; little or no work has been done on them. Belize is a poor country, but proudly solvent, owing no international debts. The civilization that flourished was supported by the agriculture of a rich river valley. This small temple—only the guard doesn't call it small—was a major site on the river, a major influence. It is still the highest building in Belize. He gazes proudly at its 130-foot height, its grassy, heavily vegetated terraces. Only a path for climbing and the top have been cleared. From its crenelated crown the British Army keeps a twenty-four-hour-a-day watch, staring over the vast expanse of forest toward the Guatemalan border. Our more ambitious members file up the grassy path, call down from the top, take pictures of us below. We wave back, take pictures of them above. They make friends with the British Army, scan through their powerful telescopes, see no Guatemalan troops advancing.

I have climbed Mayan temples. In 1960—my knees were more limber then—I used to scrabble up and down the half-cleared terraces of the Main Plaza at Tikal that the University of Pennsylvania was excavating; watch, evenings, the parrots come in to roost, listen to howler monkeys howl and storm the branches of the great trees rising above me. I went to Tikal other times too, usually in freight planes, seated on stacks of lumber. In the Yucatan, at Chichen Itza, I once found myself alone with a terrified woman. She had managed to climb to the high Temple of the Jaguar with no trouble but couldn't bring herself even to start down the narrow corridor of steep inside steps. Her companions had gone without her. Step by step, one by one, all the long dark way, I had to coax and manage her, bumping her along on her buttocks. I don't feel any need to climb Xunantunich in today's blazing heat, so I stretch out on a bench and let Dora's and the guide's words drift over me. There are a lot of things you don't have to do in this world, though it may take you years to arrive at this wisdom.

It is not a busy Park, even on a Sunday. A few young people clatter up in an ancient truck, inspect the map, patronize the water fountain. Our people straggle down, patronize the water fountain. We set our baskets in the cars and start for home, somnolent and silent.

You are forgetting—we forgot too—that this is Belize, with few roads, few cars on the roads, where whatever can happen will. Like the other day when we had three flat tires on one car in an hour, any repair shops sixty miles away. Never mind that story, it was dull. It wasn't until evening that the two of us—one was me—left to guard our stranded transportation were told that the only two buildings in sight had been the Home for Delinquent Boys (they came to investigate us but we didn't know they were delinquent) and the Insane Asylum.

Today we fortunately aren't too far from home, there is a big clatter, we look behind to see that our manifold has become separated from its moorings and is lying in the road.

I guess you need a manifold. The other car is able to avoid it and Dave, that blessed Dave who is always unhappily driving, always the one to solve our mechanical dilemmas, gets out. A master of invention, he goes looking for, and finds, a suitable sapling. Somehow he shores the pipe up in relatively its necessary position. He produces cord from the gear on our roof, loops it around each end of the sapling, passes the cord ends through the windows. Our strongest hands clutch them in a sort of tug of war and we make it back to Parrots' Wood.

"Boston," he sighs to me as I hand him a rum drink. "How soon can I get back to you and my wife? And my own car?"

While we were absorbing culture Diane had been to the City. Courtesy of our Radio Lady? She has returned with the laundry, which goes out stuffed into big sacks and returns only slightly moist. In my housekeeping role I pull it out now and pile it—sheets and towels; jeans, shirts, underwear by sex. I am ringed by snatching hands.

"That's MINE." Inevitably a sock is missing, or a pair of jeans. Gone forever. Unclaimed articles sit on our long eating table—a T-shirt, underpants—until some foggy morning Diane threatens to use them for windshield wiping. Miraculously they are claimed. Face cloths are the most to disappear, as one little lady points out. She is a librarian, neat as a pin, who curls her hair each night.

"How am I to wash the back of my neck?" she wails tonight.

A circle of astonished faces bends upon her. Working in the field all day, smeared with repellent and mosquitoes, out in the dark, home in the dark, who worries about the back of necks?

The men have grown beards. I must say, they come to table astonishingly neat. The women's hats—a balance for the beards?—are an entertaining mixture, they come to table too. Golf hats, fashionable sombreros, bandanas, peaked fishing caps—they are as motley as their owners. Jeans are pushed into woollen socks against snakes and chiggers, ticks, biting flies, whatever other dangers may lurk. It is easy to judge the experience of either sex by the simplicity and age of their attire— a casual lack of elegance which in itself is elegance, however the back of their necks.

Note: Having for twenty years survived chiggers, black flies, ticks, and bedbugs, I too am casual. Or lazy. (Certainly not elegant.) Pride goeth before a fall. Six weeks after my return from Belize I was again making a bird survey in Arizona for The Nature Conservancy, on my third mountain ranch. I was 150 miles from medical assistance, my rural mailbox 17 miles down the road, which gives you an idea of my isolation. A visitor had to excise two botfly larvae from my back. With her fingernails, lacking other equipment. Botfly eggs are transferred by mosquitoes, ticks, damp laundry, or anything else handy to their hosts, in this case me. They grow to a fair size, keeping a pipeline open to the air, keeping a feeling of discomfort and anxiety in their hostess. I couldn't reach or even see mine. Arizona Jim, a biologist, popped these unwanted guests into a beer bottle with a spoonful of preservative rum so they could be identified at the hospital in Tucson, so I could take them home to that Cape Cod doctor who had treated me for "an insignificant infection."

I don't always lead such an unkempt life. Back home if you meet me at our small post office, at market, working here or there as a volunteer, I resemble any other senior citizen. My hair is cut, sometimes I even wear a dress. (If I am in my malodorous tern or gull-spattered jeans and T-shirt, wind-blown and thirsty from banding on a beach, I hope you won't meet me.) Most of those who know me socially or see me only at meetings don't really know what I do in my spare time. "Something about birds" is as far as they get.

"Ornithological research" is the phrase for my hobby I once grandly came up with, at a dinner of the prestigious Society of Woman Geographers (the distaff side of The Explorers' Club). We were eating in splendor, two hundred of us, on the top floor of the National Geographic Society's handsome building in Washington. Members were colorfully arrayed in costumes from countries where they had climbed mountains, planted flags, dug bones, botanized, studied native cultures at close hand. In a proper dress, not my beach T-shirt and shorts, I was seated by a Senator (shortly moved to the head table, to my relief. I'm not very political). Her replacement cordially asked me what I did, what had brought me into the member-ship. I didn't feel I could stutter—it would have come out a stutter—that I "banded birds." In those days, and certainly in that awesome company, I was shy. Heads turned as I hesi-tated—the card on my bosom marked me as a new member. The second drink I had had downstairs came to my rescue. Chin up, Mrs. Fisk. That's Margaret Mead at the next table, the Navy Band piped you into the elevator. Brad would be astounded to see you sitting here.

"Ornithological research," I came out with, in a voice fairly firm. "I work in Florida." This latter statement changed the subject enough so I could retire into my dinner. Florida is a state that always provokes conversation (if not conservation).

Day 22

It is raining again, a steady, insistent rain from low rolls of gray clouds, mist fogging the pine trees; like rain in the Adirondacks. We do what we would have done in those northern mountains—lie on our beds reading, sleeping, writing, gossiping, half-lazy, half-bored. June reports she has found and photographed a strangler fig just starting its deadly embrace about its supporting tree. Birds or wind carry a seed of this parasite, lodge it in a crotch or bromeliad, where it sprouts, drops long shoots to the ground, roots. The twisting stem that results thickens, years later has strangled and obliterated its host.

These are so common in the tropics that I barely give them a glance, but Kodak has made a mint of money from them. I tell June about the enormous one at Mahogany Hammock in Everglades National Park that attracts photographers like nectar-seeking insects. (Tourists don't think of themselves as insects, though their social habits may have much in common.) Tourists also often don't notice the always-present Red-shouldered hawk that sits in a branch of the biggest mahogany tree in the United States, unless both have been lost to a hurricane since my day. Probably. They don't hear the chuck-will's-widow that calls from the boardwalk railing at dusk. Birdwatchers do, with delight. And should you be at the Hammock very early in the morning, and are as lucky as I was on my very first trip, the Sandhill cranes might come bugling over the sawgrass, flying low, trailing their long legs just over your head. Aldo Leopold saw them on the Colorado Delta—"the wildest of living fowl . . . from the far reaches of the years I see them wheeling still." As I do.

I had been sent to count immature eagles, presumed to perch in the pines near the Hammock until the morning sun set up its currents and set them rising to circle lazily in the thermals. I hadn't been told to take a telescope, so I hunted the eagles in vain, but the sight of those cranes, numenon of the new wilderness I had come to, their bugle calls, kept me from any feeling of failure. I was new in South Florida then—everything I saw was a wonder and an excitement. It's too bad that when you stay in a place you lose that sense of wonder. It's what happens to a child, growing up. Rachel Carson titled a book on it. You grow more useful to others as your experience increases, but you lose something very special to yourself. And, if you are able to communicate, to those others. Maybe you have started on the downward slide when you can no longer communicate what matters to you. I licked this by going to Arizona. I loved my years in South Florida, though—shaking dew from my nets at moonset, still working at moonrise, extracting catbirds.

I have gathered an audience. There are no secrets in this house, every footfall, every whisper is evident. The people downstairs have joined us on our beds. I have finished mending the rips in Diane's shirt and am telling them about the early days of Manomet Bird Observatory, where I was involved from its beginning because its Director (Kathleen Anderson, lazing on her own bed over at the Main House) thought I was my medical daughter-in-law, and might assist her on an encephalitis project. That first summer I had lived alone in the big, creaky summer house, east winds blowing my curtains at night, seabirds crying below the steep bluff. I was in charge of a half-mile or more of mist nets, running them early in the morning, supervising the volunteers who came to learn during the days, then working alone along the paths through the woods until dark. When Kathleen went off camping with her husband (I am in favor of women camping, or anything else with their husbands), I substituted for her the next few years until a proper staff was built up. Then I became a Trustee, but what gets discussed in Trustee Meetings is finances, fund-raising, problems. What I like is to be free in the field, wind and leaves blowing about me, not about a table full of figures and cigarette butts: birds or flowers or wormy apples in my hand rather than reports. Kathleen joined our first two ornithological expeditions to Belize, working with Dora.

"All very well," Amy breaks in impatiently, "but how did you become a bird bander? Not just a backyard bander but this sort of—of professional amateur, in the first place? The people you have worked with are legends to our generation. How did you get mixed up with them?"

It's a long story, it would bore them. So on a pretext I slip away for a walk, the drip is coming now only from the trees, not from the torn sky. The Western Highway is full of puddles. Alone I can go at my own pace. I stop to watch a butterfly hunt an opening flower, a small brown bird scuttle under a bush, an arc of swallows pursuing their suppers against the sky. No need to murmur "hmmmm, hmmmm" as someone talks. Why don't we have more respect for silence? There is so much to listen to. Even indoors when we stop talking for a moment there is the creak of wood, the drip and splash of rain outside, the different squeaks of mattresses as we move on them.

Evening

I have been scribbling in this notebook since the day we arrived. Tonight for the first time I am asked—

"WHAT are you writing in there, all the time?"

Dessert plates have completed their circuit, coffee mugs have been refilled. Sometimes I think I am invisible. At meals I have as much on my tongue as the next person. *I* think my stories are amusing, but there never seems to be an opening I can crash into to tell them. So I listen, watch reactions, the developments of friendship or friction. Everyone needs an audience; I comfort myself—maybe this is my role.

The woman who asks this question knows my scribbling can't possibly be the scientific, careful details she herself commits to paper each evening; often I haven't even been out in the forest that day. Besides, she has known my casual ways for fifteen years, we are old colleagues. Actually for once I *am* making notes, on a Gray hawk we found nesting this morning. Dora was delighted, she has little information on the species. Everyone had to get out of the cars, climb a hill, look through a telescope to verify this bird. I am sketching the location for her, and the mileage, so she can keep the nest under surveillance.

I say this. My questioner knows it is not the whole truth but does not pursue her inquiry. Afraid to probe beneath the crust, to find the real person alive in there? Out of courtesy?

What tide holds us together, this conglomeration of iceberg tips in a wide ocean?

"Why did you stop?" I ask in my turn. "Or was that just a polite question to indicate you know I'm sitting beside you?"

Janet laughs. "I was being delicate. I should know better with you."

We discuss why people back off. We discuss—we have taken our coffee outside—our companions. We decide they affect us like music. Some flow about us almost unheard, some set our feet to dancing, some demand the application of intellect, of effort, to be appreciated. And some strike emotional levels in us that can vary from happiness to pain, to depths, unexpectedly, we do not wish uncovered. We back off from these, but we return, we are bonded to them. By what? Janet fetches more coffee and we discuss this too. How what you hear and perceive in a person on Tuesday is not what you may see or hear on Thursday. The one truth, we all decide—others have joined us—is that the longer you listen the more complex the music, the person, becomes, and so the richer our living.

"And now," demands Janet again of me, laughing again, "what *is* it you write every night in that blue notebook we gave you for bird observations? Tell me!"

I hug it, closed, to my breast. "I don't want to," I tell her, laughing also. "Next year? I promise. You first."

She looks at me quizzically, grants me the right to my privacy. Then outside a big cat crosses the lawn in front of us, in full moonlight.

Problems go with pretending to be an expert. When the excitement dies down, my roommates cluster about me. Dora and Diane have gone off on some errand.

"Jonnie, do cats attack people?"

I have to tell them I don't know. "I suppose it depends on how hungry they are. In Arizona the rancher told me I needn't worry about mountain lions (pumas). They eat cattle but are only curious about humans. They may come close to you, follow you, but will not attack. I was alone a lot, the rancher may have been trying to keep me from worrying. I never heard of an attack, but I suppose the victims aren't in shape to talk about it. In Florida a bobcat once walked right under my hand on a narrow path, as if I didn't exist. I could have stroked its ears but thought it best not to. It had been hand raised by a woman, though, which would make a difference, would have conditioned it."

Other bobcats passed through that Biological Station, wild ones. Some had been trapped and radio-collared. The graduate student monitoring them from his truck told me one had her territory just off one of my net lanes. To his surprise she didn't even move when I passed. I was vexed. I wanted her to move, I wanted to see her. I found her scat, but that was hardly the same thrill.

When our real experts return, Dora admits she has seen a puma, or a jaguar, she wasn't sure which. She has found prints in the mud near our cottage, but our feet had trampled them and she couldn't be sure of their size. She had thought it best not to worry us. I notice that Diane, who walks that path alone when we are not here, says little. She is in the forest more than Dora, working with her survival expeditions, but she offers no stories. Since two of the women are anxious, they suggest that for the few nights remaining perhaps we should be driven around to the house at bedtime, we can march down the path from the road in a group. I count us quickly. There will be one too many for the car. I should *love* to see a cat on our path, in the shadows. (Would I, really?) That winter I had spent mostly alone on a remote mountain, my Nature Conservancy sponsors had worried.

"At my age," I had assured them, "I am expendable. My grandchildren will remember me far longer and more colorfully if I am eaten by a coyote or a mountain lion than if I die in bed. Or in a highway accident, which, with all the driving I do, is more probable.

Here, I suppose, if Grandmother is attacked by a cat she will be shortly found, carted off to the Mennonite hospital. It will be inconvenient. But since I am considerably bigger than the dogs that jaguars are reputed to take, I decide to take my chances on that path. With a flashlight. This cat must have been around all month. Nothing but ticks have attacked us.

Day 23

I sulked in my tent all morning. (That's about all I remember from my years of classical study in that proper school for young ladies in Boston—that Achilles sulked in his tent; I don't know why. I didn't learn much at that school. I was a whiz at basketball, though.)

I don't know why I am sulking, either, unless my digestion is rebelling against the steady heat and humidity here. Or against that peanut butter I ate too much of yesterday? Against getting up so early in the mornings to start off somewhere when we never leave until an hour after announced departure time? This morning I went out early on a transect. We had only two hummingbirds, unidentified; one warbler, heard only. Not much to report for a two-mile slog. My companion, who has also stayed for both sessions of this Tropical Adventure, agrees, also somewhat sulkily, that one session might have been enough. Our excitement at the novelty has died. Twenty years ago we were as wide-eyed and enthusiastic as the newcomers seeing "exotic" birds.

"Resident, not exotic," my fellow-complainer corrected the neophyte bouncing along with us. She had come on the transect eager to add life birds to her list, kept asking the names of flowers and trees, was thrilled by what to us is no longer an adventure. "Exotic birds are ones foreign to a country. These birds live here."

Actually I am surly—I force myself to look at myself, at reality—because it is time I found something new to work at, and I don't know what. Maybe my patron Saint, Anthony, will slip something into my mail. The newcomers have brought us stories of storms, closed highways, and airports they were glad to leave behind. Today I would gladly trade these against the enervating heat, the warnings of deeper mud, more insects where we are to work tomorrow. My age is showing. This upsets my digestion too.

In spite of which I eat a hearty breakfast of papaya, eggs scrambled with onion, tomatoes and peppers, two slices of my cinnamon bread, two cups of coffee. I refuse the offers of Lomotil and Pepto Bismol my housemates have (in abundance) in their luggage; stretch out on my green and orange sheets that depict jungles and jaguars and go back to sleep. I will make up for the time I missed abed by going on that transect.

Later I hang my wet and muddy jeans on the fence, wash my muddy socks, set my wet and muddy sneakers in the sun, sort my belongings, finish the book I have been reading a few pages at a time, and wish I were at home reading my galley proofs, which will by now be awaiting my attention. There *must* be something wrong with my digestion. Where is my gay and cheery self, savoring every minute?

The creamy racemes of the mango trees near Jaime's garden have gone by. In Florida when groves were heavy with their blossoms the sales of Kleenex mushroomed. Maybe their pollen was the cause of my allergy the other day? I had been careful to stay away from them, but it was hard, as they are always full of warblers snacking on the insects about those lovely flowers.

Today a feathery tree with a profusion of delicate branching blooms attracts orioles. The females and young are the same greenish-yellow as the flowers, hard to separate from them. At lunch the tree is visible from the table. I am eating with another woman who has stayed home from the forest. She keeps asking me the names of things, and I can't help her.

"But you have been in these countries so often," she murmurs cattily. "Haven't you learned the names?"

No, I haven't. I should have. My mind wanders instead of filing what I see and hear in neat pigeonholes. I am cross with myself for this but not to the point of reforming. Then I remember my mother and am cheered. She too was provoked one day by such questions. It was I who was asking them.

"Do you have to know the name of something to enjoy it?" she rebuked me. "Can't you just listen to it, look at it? Must I know the numbers of those Mozart sonatas you try to play before I take pleasure in them?"

Bully for Mama! I sit up straighter. I point out to my heckler the several different vines intertwined on the screen outside our porch, a hummingbird (I DO know the name of that) hovering at the tubular flowers. I distract her. I show her Dora's long shelf of scientific books that can answer her questions if she wishes to take the time. But she is unused to the humidity, goes off to take a nap. As do I. Another one.

I *am* restless. I haven't enough to do here. I should have gone home last week. (And where could I have been fitted in the cars?) I've started a letter, I've been scribbling in this notebook again, but you can't write—I can't—unless you are upbeat. So now I am out on the old road, walking off my ill humor. Not very successfully.

What you need to write about in a letter or a journal, what you let your friends see, if you want to have friends, are the bright coins of your days—the small happinesses, the uneventful minutiae that can be turned into laughter, illuminations, the courtesies and goodness of your companions. The other side of those coins, which keep psychiatrists in business—the Why Am I Here? Who Wants Me? What Makes Me Think I Matter?—we try to conceal. Who wants to hear your problems? They have their own. Who wants to read them spread out on paper? I have been reading such a book, by a woman always in tears. Why doesn't she shape up? I ask crossly as I plod through her pages. What good is all that crying doing her, or me? There has to be something immoral about her making money from it.

Those groups that get together, reaching out to touch someone and be supportive—my niece keeps urging me to join one, sends me clippings about them. They sit around holding hands, expatiating on their unhappinesses, wiping away each other's tears. Perhaps there are a lot of them in California, where she lives; I never hear about them in Tucson or Colorado or frosty New England, where people are too busy, maybe, coping with weather. As far as I can make out, it isn't the real sorrows of life they seek comfort for, but the inadequacies that plague us all, the losses that nibble at our self-esteem. Do we need to hang these out on the line? Most people I know, if they reach out to touch someone, find the family dog or cat arching under their hand, hungry. Or a neighbor's child, also hungry; a goat or a cow in need of attention. Instead of their own troubled image in the mirror, it is someone else they must take care of. And, oddly enough, this takes care of them. Instead of being locked, their doors are open to the neighborhood, to the world.

Having said this, I remember we are living in a fenced compound.

Anyway—I kick at a log I have just tripped over, I am still

in bad humor—I am reading two of these self-serving books, one by a man, one by a woman. Maybe they will teach me something, how people like this solve their problems. Because I have them too, as do you.

When someone comes to us for comfort, is it curiosity that makes us listen, or the flattering of our ego because we think we can help them? An opportunity to pontificate? Do we feel useful when we let them burrow their brows in our shoulder? (Someday we may need to reciprocate.) They had better not bring their buckets to our well too often, or they will find the spring drained.

Psychiatrists, I suppose, listen to our woes because it is their living. I've often wondered what nourishes a minister's compassion. A doctor going out at midnight has a broken leg to set, a baby to deliver. A minister just has some parishioner who can't cope. Well, maybe a broken mental spring is as serious as a broken leg. It's harder to deal with, that's for sure. And I guess I'd like, often, like today, to have someone hold my hand, soothe me into thinking that I am a Big Girl, that what I do and don't think is important. It isn't, but we are all in this world together. We might as well put on the best face we can, be cheerful, laugh the way Dora does so contagiously, feed people well, pick up behind them. Listen. Keep our mouths closed. Keep our coins bright side up. Sympathy leads to compassion, compassion to love, and love, they say, is what makes the world go round. I kick at another log. What I could use right now is someone to love me.

As you can see, the coin of this hour of my afternoon is tarnished. Probably I am hungry. Or weary, and unwilling to admit it. Fatigued by the heat. Besides, there is no one around to trade cheerful stories with, only that woman who wants to know names.

I take an orange, a book, my binoculars and go to sit by the pond, where a broken pump makes a comfortable backrest. There is a fine view of the mango trees and the bushes along the verge where small birds forage. It is sunny and peaceful.

Emerald and ruby, a pair of parrots noisily squawk their way over the water. Usually they fly so fast I can't determine the species, but these settle nearby, the male bending his head to show off his yellow crown. I must be invisible, leaning so still against the pump. My betters tell me impatiently that the Yellow-lored has a red patch in his wings, but how can I observe everything at once? That red shows only in flight. Besides, their harsh calls unsettle me. The Yellow-lored are the commonest, coming for seeds of the wild calliandra, so Dora orders her men to leave this wild shrub uncut. The locals think all English are crazy, she says comfortably, so they obey her. And that all Americans are English.

I drop my orange peels into the pond. In Florida orange growers feed oranges to their cattle when the groves freeze or the price is not right. Will fish also eat them? Yes, a flurry of silver bodies flicker momentarily at the surface, then they and the skins disappear in the murk. A large, lemon-yellow butterfly lands beside me on a melastoma leaf, failing to recognize me as a threat. With wings folded it is a perfect mimic, in size and color; its wings even are striated. It's not a heliconia, though there are many of these here. My favorite has a crimson slash on its forewings, a white bar across the hind.

Martins sweep high after invisible insects, swing low to bathe on the wing, shaking drops of water from their feathers as they rise. The song of a Spot-breasted wren bursts from a bush. That's a small, plump bird I once chased down in Tobago trying to attach its joyous music to its unseen singing throat. It sounded, I had told those I was guiding, the way I felt inside when I was happy. How long since I have had joy like that bubbling in my throat? I brush the question aside, thrust it down under the peace of this hour.

I change position to watch an acorn woodpecker climb the stub of an ancient, hurricane-twisted pine. Another emerges from a hole at the top, they confer, he pops into the hole. (The pattern of the forehead sexes them for me.) I glimpse another head at the hole. Acorns stay in family groups, help each other at the nest. Below them an epiphyte is wound around the trunk of this survivor (I'm talking about the tree, not the woodpecker), almost as big as its host. It isn't a strangler fig, but it has grown from some small seed, windblown or deposited by a bird in a moist crotch or clump of fern, where frogs also cling. Surprisingly, at just the right moment our botanist comes hurrying across our little bridge, very businesslike. Where was she at lunch when I needed her? I interrupt her passage to ask the name of the epiphyte, but her mind is elsewhere. She has heard a radio warning of a great wind in Belize City headed our way. She wants to reach the men, working a mile away.

"Don't forget your book," she warns me in her teacherly way, noticing it neglected by the pump. I return to my platform and await the wind, which does not arrive. Never believe a weatherman.

I also return to the acorn woodpeckers. In an Arizona canyon one fall day I had watched a pair steadily fly back and forth to the sheltered porch of a cabin. My companion and I trespassed, finding the cabin shingles precisely studded with row on row of acorns, firmly imbedded. The owners of the cabin, finding us at their doorstep, told us that some of these emergency rations protruded right into their living room. At the moment these provided an extra sheathing, but by February they wondered if wind might not whistle through the holes?

They were not offended by our trespassing. Most birders are happy to share their enthusiasms. Maybe it is a difference between indoor and outdoor people? I have been put down often by academic scientists, who speak a special language, who can be impatient with those who don't. Perhaps it is because they must spend their time indoors with no opportunity to lift their eyes unto the hills. Perhaps they are warped, made sharp-tongued by this frustration? On the other hand, astronomers on windswept hills, geologists inexplicably tapping on rocks in a pasture have shared their knowledge, their telescopes, and their tools with me. Their activities were no more odd to them, and to me, than someone studying a bird through binoculars. It's only when you see birders clustered about telescopes on a beach, or a group peering up into a tree, that they become subjects for cartoonists.

Our botanist's bustling energy has depressed me. I don't seem to have any energy, today or yesterday. I am doing what I want to do (I don't want to do anything) and am taking no pleasure in it. WHAT is wrong with me? To cheer myself as I dangle my feet over the water, I watch a small yellow bird with a black line through its eye. I dig into the pocket of my past and run between my fingers a handful of stones of differing shapes and textures—worry beads you might call them, strung into a loose necklace. Or a litany. Is this a correct use of that musical word *litany?* Yes, it derives from the Greek, means an *en-treating.* I am entreating comfort, here by this afternoon's pond, from the friends who have carried me on my way these ornithological years. Joe, Bill—three Bills: one gray-eyed, humorous, searching for and always finding the exact illuminating word; one dynamic and generous, hassling me into action; the third an artist working patiently in the hot space of a motor home. All three took me into their separate wildernesses, let me work with them, traded the energy of my arms and legs for visions of what motivated them. This stone is Mitch, who would needle the Queen of England if they sat together at dinner. I wonder what he said to St. Peter as he passed him, the night he was liberated at last from pain? But he wouldn't have passed Peter, he would have stopped to talk, to ask questions, to assay possibilities for heavenly photography. . . . Here is Fred, gentle, frustrated, with eyes that see through pretense but keep bitterness to themselves; Major, who taught me waterskiing and a bittern's cry; Cal with his Georgia drawl. Each one a teacher, a friend to whom I may return, affection between us. Young John, eager, on his way up, never too busy to help me, coming to me when he needed help. Old John, weary, wise, given to drinking whiskey. Sandy and Gene, guarding me between them on our flight halfway around a continent. I roll their names under my tongue, the vignettes they evoke making me laugh or sigh.

There were women, but peripheral. Oddly women don't come to you for help in the same way—not to me, anyway, nor me to them. I don't know why. There is affection between us but the bars never go all the way down, the cards don't get set out on the table in the same way. Perhaps because we talk over soup or coffee rather than over a drink, our inhibitions are not breached?

It was the men I craved, as a widow; their deep voices, their willingness to include me, their objective interests. They were fifteen, twenty, thirty years younger than I. These days—well, never mind! Their memories are the stones I rub, polish in my pocket, balancing them against the deep and still abiding love I lost. Doesn't everyone wake in the small night hours, seeking reassurance, reaching for some sort of worry beads? We all grope our ways, need love. With Brad my heart spilled over with warmth and happiness. After he was gone I watched that warmth dessicate. I was like a tree still standing straight and tall—pride kept me tall—its inside burned out by lightning. I said that before, it's a good analogy.

Then, as a dead tree offers shelter and nourishment to wildlife, slowly—it took years—I attracted a new family, sent out new roots. The biologists I had joined dragged me into their interests, whether crocodiles, shore birds, or trips to tropical countries, always adventurous. They taught me to handle tools, change fuses, drive trucks. Hourly and casually these men opened doors on worlds I hadn't known existed, in which I could immerse myself. I tried to be equally casual so they wouldn't recognize my ignorance. When they did, as long as I provided useful arms and legs and my handwriting was legible, they didn't seem to care. I tried not to talk too much. I brought cookies—biologists are always hungry. I brimmed with honest admiration, I was too old to worry their wives. It was an ideal situation and I certainly made the most of it.

Shadows have moved over the pond. It is time to light lamps for those who will come straggling back, time to pick up the book I haven't opened, to see what Diane has put into tonight's stew. Relaxed and content, I leave the martins curving in flight against the sunset sky. I drop my worry beads, those polished stones of friendship, back into their pocket until I shall need them again.

Day 24

At sunset I slip off for a walk; I have been with people all day. I go up the path past the outhouse, past the clump of trees where everyone has seen a Grace's warbler but me, for whom it would be a life bird, cross the planks over a ditch, am at the old Western Road. This slants up, given a curve or two, to the highway a mile distant. Dead center above it, huge and golden, a globe of light glowing and glorious in a sky also golden, hangs Venus, the evening star. A light footfall sounds behind me. It is Diane on the solitary walk that frees her from the duties that pile on her each day. Neither of us speaks. She passes with her dancer's step, her long skirt swinging about her ankles, a slim figure growing smaller, disappearing around a curve toward home so that Venus and I are again alone.

The gold pales, stars prick out in a scattering of light, it is an empty world, a magic hour.

Coming toward me down the rise, only a silhouette as shadows thicken, I see a man. He will be a hunter, out for agouti or paca, to feed his family. The subconscious has extraordinary power. Instantly I have swung around. Beyond reason, I am panicked. Not daring to run, not daring to look over my shoulder to see how much closer that lone figure has come.

Walking on a similar road in Mexico last year, again at dusk, I had survived a rape attempt. Of *me?* A crone in her seventies, in rain, wrapped in a slicker? The scene still makes me laugh. But only on the surface I learn now as I try to out-race those steps behind me.

That Mexican expedition, unexpected, hasty, full of mis-adventure from its beginning, was—well, different from my other forays. It had started with a call to me in Arizona, where I was winding down a survey in Aravaipa Canyon. By merest chance I was in Tucson overnight. A firm, pleasant voice, giv-ing a name I didn't recognize, said he understood I knew trop-ical birds and spoke Spanish. He wondered if I might be willing to join him in a study of wintering North American warblers in an area of Mexico he had worked seven years before. He hoped to assess the affect on migrant populations of forest destruction and was quite desperate for assistance.

Well, why not? It sounded interesting, I liked his voice.

"Only I can't come this week," I told him. "I haven't fin-ished what I am doing here. My Spanish isn't that good, either."

He had laughed, set a date I could manage, rung off. As I have said, I often select my companions by their voices on the phone, that being all I have to go by. Sometimes I am wrong, but he proved, on our closely-tied acquaintance in often diffi-cult circumstances, to be a man as companionable—and as firm—as his voice. Young. I tried one night to use my longer years of experience, my training in foreign countries, to per-suade him of the difference between firmness and stubborness, but only learned (again) that you don't change people, you must love them for what they are. If you insist on loving them. I have a loving heart: nicked, but what matter?

At the last moment his colleague from the Smithsonian, who was to accompany and guide me, canceled, so that I descended from my plane that evening in a small Mexican airport with no instruction of where I was to go, or how. Somehow—the circumstances were incredible, too complex to narrate—my new associate and I missed each other. The airport was closing for the night, I was locked in by a torrential downpour. St. Anthony, patron of all lost objects, always kind to me, came to my rescue. Miraculously—it was entirely a miracle—we encountered each other, survived hours of navigation through flooded country roads. At two in the morning I was pushed into a small room already occupied by a pair of newlyweds (so there was an extra bed available). This tempo continued through our daily rounds. The people who collected about our nucleus would make a book in themselves. I never had time, or the strength, to take notes.

Storms—*nortes*—sluiced in over the coastal ranges, dropped their burdens from the sea day after day. Much of my time was spent in a forest; I had little chance to go birding on the open road near the motel where we slept. Finally, late one afternoon, wrapped in my old green slicker, I managed. I had daily seen a hawk in a field nearby, I wanted to get near enough to identify it. I went out alone. A handsome young fisherman in a scarlet shirt fell in with me, walked me along in friendly conversation until we were out of sight of the fishermen's village where he lived, then tried to rape me. We were almost within screaming distance of our primitive quarters, where I might have been heard, but it never occurred to me to scream, I was laughing too hard. Probably what saved me was my laughter, as well as the stout leather belt fastening my jeans, its buckle not evident. I wasn't frightened. His choice of me at my age, muddy, hooded, seemed to me hilarious. I pointed out in my best Spanish that I was surely older than his *abuela*. In our tussles, our thrashing about on the ground, my eyeglasses didn't even get broken. He settled at last for ripping my wristwatch and my binoculars bloodily off me. These were retrieved the next day in a Mack Sennett comedy, with fishermen, fat policemen with rifles, our motel owner, my colleague, and a Mexican student who had joined our research— and me, timidly tailing—sneaking single-file through the huts of the fishing village. Dealing with bureaucracy took longer. Rape seemed not to be too serious a crime in Mexico, but my fisherman had a record as a horse thief, which was. Another woman's watch, expensive (mine was a Timex), turned up in his wallet. I had to wonder what had happened to her. I learned later that after we left the hawk field was bulldozed for planting and thirty human bodies, some only recently dead, were uncovered. St. Anthony had been watching over me that day.

I had thought the incident left me unscarred. It made an amusing dinner-table story for a while. Then I noticed that while women were always curious, men shied off from my telling, so I dropped it, forgot it. I had plenty of other stories from that trip to laugh over. But tonight at dusk the scar breaks open. I am out of control on that broken road, not daring to run.

I make it back to our path with its obscuring hedge of bushes. Our cottage shows welcome light, I hear the voices of my friends. The man continued down the road. My heart slowly stops pounding. At the Main House no one notices me. I am left to reflect on the strength of the subconscious and to wonder, shuddering as I sip a stiffer rum than usual, when the next such occurrence may surface.

Day 25

The days have not taught me wisdom. Not enough, anyway. I *am* wise enough not to go today to Crooked Tree Lagoon far, far away. It will be a long ride, then hours of sitting in an open boat baking in the sun if the sun is out, soaking in rain if the rain comes down. Depending on the water level and the food supply, the Lagoon will be full of waterbirds. Dora and Meg are trying to get it made into a preserve. I was flown over that Lagoon in a small plane, cruised it in an airboat a few years ago on a survey for the Prime Minister being made by our National Audubon Society. It is similar to our Everglades before they became crisscrossed by highways and airboat trails and sugar industries. I lived with waterbirds my winters in Florida, did my own crisscrossing. There are exotic creatures here, though, that the Everglades lack—jabiru storks, boat-billed herons, lizards of different sorts and sizes. I should be more ambitious. Instead I wave the cars off. One is hired, we don't dare send the green Nova that far. The occupants are armed with Pepto Bismol, sun lotion, cans of insect repellent, binoculars, cameras, telescopes, hats, raincoats, and lunch—in order of importance and their physical conditions.

I eat a leisurely breakfast, arm myself with my own repel-

lent, binoculars, an orange and set off for the river, promising
Diane to be back in time to join her in the kitchen. Last night's
cornbread has been demolished.

The river is further than you think, yesterday's hikers told
me, but the water is clean, no one is there, you can strip and
swim. You can't get lost, just go straight.

I can always get lost. A cart lane leads through what would
never qualify as an orchard in our country, just a few scraggly
cashew trees raggedly spaced, hurricane leavings. I obey
instructions and go straight. I should LOOK at what I am
doing. The track narrows, the grass grows taller, becomes scrub,
becomes second growth impossibly tangled. Then I can't push
further unless I bend double, cats have made this trail. The
only river is of sweat running down my nose and back. I started
this as a pleasure jaunt, not a stubborn endurance test. I
remember, rather late, the warnings of reptiles and start to
watch where I set my sneakers, to step carefully over logs. I
remember the pills my M.D. has ordered me to carry at all
times. I remember the water bottle I forgot to bring.

Back by the cashews, not leading straight ahead at all, I
find the bootmarks of yesterday's couple in the mud and then—
Oh Joy! clearly defined cat tracks, both large and small, crossed
by the sharp hoofs of a little Brocket deer. I am back in the
open, a breeze cools me, the cats went all along this muddy
lane. On my return I'll sketch and measure their prints.

I come to an orange grove, its white blossoms fragrant among
nascent dark globes of fruit. An almost-ripe one slakes my
thirst. The path angles off through head-high grass (full of
ticks, I shortly discover), leads out to a small, untidy milpa.
A milpa is a clearing made by hacking down forest hardwoods,
burning them for their potash, planting a few bananas, some
corn. There is not enough to feed a family in this one, it is

just a gesture, its burned tree trunks scattered like jackstraws. If there is a river here, I think, hot again, brushing the tall grass from my eyes—suddenly it is at my feet, pouring swiftly around a curve below a steep bank. Opaque green, the shadows of pan-sized fish moving in it, a kingfisher rattling under the overhanging trees whose shade is welcome.

I consider swimming, but the bank is a sheer drop of red mud. Easier to look at the flow, float instead on the current of cool air that rises from it. If that current carried me around the bend how would I get back? The water is doubtless full of those minnows, cousins of piranhas, that kept us thrashing in Blue Creek last year if we weren't to emerge rashed by bites. So I spread my slicker—never move without a slicker—and sit. Small birds return to branches about me. I might be there yet, with notebook and binoculars, far from the outside world, peaceful.

Peace is rare—life trips you up. Just as well I hadn't stripped to swim. On the far side of the river a disturbance resolves itself into two young men and a cur dog moving about a dugout canoe on the bank. They are washing, I decide. Clothes? Selves? The cur runs up and down. I must be clearly visible if they look. Yesterday's hikers reported they had encountered two men, Spanish speaking. Belizeans speak English. Probably they were Guatemalans or Salvadorans who had infiltrated the border, Diane said. Living off forest animals, cutting small milpas. Possibly guerrillas, Dora said; they are in the forest these days too. Both had glanced at the Dobermans. To have survived the violence of their countries, escaped across the border, refugees have to be tough—and rough.

Uncertain, I put my binoculars in my bag. I don't mind losing my virtue (at least I think I don't), but at today's prices I can't replace my old Zeisses. Now the men realize I am there, and female. They whistle and catcall, one of them climbs into the dugout. Again my subconscious takes over; that Mexican incident scarred me deeper than I know. Grabbing my slicker and notebook I start up the path, walking as if unalarmed as long as I am in their sight, then skittering along toward the milpa, running through the high grass so fast no tick could cling to me. It is uphill, I am panting. Where are those pills I am warned to carry?

"Don't hurry," my doctor tells me. "Pace yourself. Let the telephone ring. Avoid stress."

He doesn't believe the stories of where my bird work takes me. Seated decorously in his office, I am to him just another senior citizen with the irreversible problems of age, needing a finger stitched now and then, nothing serious. At the moment his warnings are not as strong as those leaping in my subconscious; he doesn't understand the types of stress that hit me. I run until I am breathless. I could hide in the bushes, but that cur dog would find me. I know I am being foolish, I know no one is after me. It is the violence we see daily on TV, I scold myself, those stupid mysteries I buy to read on airplanes. It is fear of the unknown. Worse, of being a mile and more from anyone I know. My feet leave no track in the grass. I don't stop to measure and sketch those cat tracks, though I am half a mile on now, safe around several bends, no dog barking in the distance, no watchdog parrots calling in the forest. Farther along, in sight of the farm house, I do stop for breath, examine fresh heron tracks in the mud, made since I passed there earlier. I wipe repellent out of my eyes where sweat has carried it.

"I am a fool. I won't *live* with you the rest of my life like this," I snarl at my subconscious. "Leave me alone!"

What else am I carrying deep inside me? How do I know

when one of my children is in trouble, when a letter I am waiting for has reached my mailbox, when something happening a mile or a continent away sends a surge of joy welling through me? It's impractical, that's what it is. Does everyone carry these springs of terror and worry and happiness within them?

When asked later about the river I downplay my fear, my race past the milpa, past the cat tracks. Why do we hesitate to talk about what really matters?

I know why.

Still Day 25. Evening

The first group returning from the Lagoon showed up late in their taxi, reporting a hair-raising drive. Dora has had trouble with her car and detoured to the City for new spark plugs. We sit out on the verandah, our feet on the railing, waiting. A full moon swims up behind the pines over the pond. I delay hunger with the story of my expedition to Belize last year. Its purpose was similar to ours, its circumstances very different. Fifteen of us had worked, slept, and eaten in an open, unisex shed lit only by three small and inefficient lamps. Washing was in a river down a steep muddy bank. The easiest way to get into this was to swing out on a rope and let go with a mighty splash. Getting out involved a crawl up through mud, so you—I, anyway—were as dirty when you finished as when you began, and maybe not in as good a humor. (I like to wash my face, mornings, and my hands off and on during the day.) Dinner daily was a deep kettle of rice and a deep kettle of beans, with a third kettle offering either plain spaghetti or instant mashed potatoes as a side dish. The poor light didn't matter, there was not too much guesswork as to what your fork lifted. A few times we had chicken, brought up flapping from the village. Next day our packaged chicken noodle soup was enriched—to the dismay of those who dredged these additions into their bowls—by the legs and feet of the previous night's dinner.

My stories make Diane's Evening Stew sound like ambrosia. Our cooking had been done over a fire on a dirt floor. A circle of rocks supported the three kettles, which also provided boiled water for tea or coffee. A huge skillet yielded breakfast eggs or, as an occasional treat, fried dough sprinkled with sugar. I watched the production of this fried dough and tried it on my return home. I must have been hungrier in the forest. . . . Our daily bread was imported, expensive, sliced U.S. Wonder loaves, until I discovered that Juanita could be cajoled, if she had time, if her husband Mario showed up to do the kneading (I was not trusted), into making a homemade variety that elicited cries of delight as it was handed up the steps to our bench-encircled table. The oven was primitive—that big skillet balanced on the circle of hot rocks, over it a piece of metal roofing holding hot coals. My back-packing friends of the North who carry an expensive assortment of dehydrated foods miss a lot in the way of exercising ingenuity. I guess what I have learned most from my various excursions into other cultures is that if you are hungry, anything tastes good. I learned to turn out pretty good French-Canadian bannock, in our fishing years. Made with lake water. Nowadays it would be flavored with acid rain . . .

When visitors came to our field station Mario would give the evening seminar, on Mayan history. He spoke excellent English, was informed and literate, his talks never twice the same. If he had ended a day's work in his fields by carrying a case of cola the mile up from the village on his shoulders, pulling against a tumpline, and had helped Juanita with the dishes we passed down to stack on the two small board tables that equipped her kitchen, he might be tired. Then he simply encouraged the visitors to ask questions.

It was hard for some urbanites to comprehend that these Indians live entirely off their land. They live inland from coastal settlements and conveniences and are independent of money. In winter when there are no fruits they simply tighten their belts. Their children, their riches, cling to the skirts of the women grinding rice in the hut doorways. Pigs root in the grassy spaces between huts, and an occasional burro, a few hens. In the river shallows by the bridge the women wash their clothes; further along, where it is more private, themselves.

"What, no indoor plumbing?" three tourist ladies from New York asked me. With a bored guide they had picked their way through the pigs and donkey droppings to peer into a hut, then found me sitting on the bridge, watching, peering at, a flight of parakeets flashing over the river.

"No outdoor either," I told them with amusement, watching their faces. They snapped their cameras at the hut, at children coming out of school, and didn't stay.

Children were everywhere. Welcome additions to their family's work force, they never begged, although often asked politely if we might have pencil or paper for them—treasures in short supply in their schools. If I sat for a moment on the bridge or on the porch of our shed, small fingers would explore the textures of my clothing, touch the comb in my hair, my wedding ring; curious, friendly.

As I talk the moon rises beyond view, its place taken by rolling clouds. Finally we serve a fine meal of black beans and rice, a local root vegetable, starchy and bland, bread, banana pudding laced with the last of the rum. If the City group doesn't arrive with a fresh supply they will have to suffer.

We eat by candlelight, the generator has ceased to function. Diane understands its difficulty, but the key to the tool kit has gone to the Lagoon in someone's pocket. We estimate the extra charge for candlelight, how much our meal would have cost in a restaurant. Moonlight, reflected from the leaves, disappears. By the time the rest of the crew arrives, (carrying rum) the station wagon purring like a kitten, a light rain is falling.

After the usual discussion of morning duties and breakfast hours—so many to go on transects, so many to be driven early to the nets—as all is settled, we are heading for bed, I ask, "And what if it's still raining?"

"Roll over and go back to sleep," orders our Leader firmly. Hopefully. He is tired. All of us who have been here a month are tired. But since it is now really Dry Season there have been few heavy showers, this second crew has not experienced the luxury of rolling over and going back to sleep.

Day 26

It rains all night. There is the usual clatter of water dripping onto our tin roof, running into the cisterns. There is a new leak over my bed; water drips onto my sneakers. So I am awake when the three ladies upstairs start pattering about at 5:30. Their activity doesn't bother me, although I wonder why they are up. I hold my tongue as they pass, going out in their yellow slickers to the biffy, but when they pass my pillow the second time with equipment bulging beneath the slickers, I ask, "Where do you think you're going, in the rain?"

None of my business; I should keep my big mouth shut. I may have special privileges, but I am not Staff. Only I know how tired those women at the Main House are at the end of a month's running this operation, the planning, feeding, procuring of supplies, endless driving, worries over driving, being at everyone's beck and call, always cheerfully. How they must have relished waking up to rain, turning over and going back to sleep!

But our ladies are itchy. They have only four days left to see, to learn, to run transects, to take birds out of nets. They don't want to miss a minute.

Shortly they return, dripping and subdued. The propane

has given out. They hadn't even been able to have coffee. They retreat upstairs and not a peep comes from them. My roommate is reading in bed, by flashlight. I too have a book, saved for emergency. In case we have a rainy day. I roll over and go back to sleep.

Later. Afternoon

The rain stops. We have visitors. For some reason they want to go, or Dora wants to take them, down Hummingbird Highway, where we are again netting, toward Dangriga. Fifty miles south. I am invited, perhaps to make up for being left out of a trip to the Blue Hole that morning; perhaps because three people in the back seat bounce less like popcorn; or perhaps just because Dora knows I enjoy being with her, am always entertained by her stories, can be counted on to provoke her to tell more.

I can't decide if this is a scenic or a birding trip. Trucks are still working at Blue Hole (they defeated the previous trip, so I needn't have been morose at missing it). We drive on. And on and on. WHAT is Dora doing? I know, although the visitors don't, that she must be back at the gas station before it closes, to pick up her spare tire. We are driving without one, which is not only risky but crazy in this country where you may not see another car for fifty miles. I am beginning to think it *will* be fifty miles if we don't reverse. I murmur about the hour, the distance. Dora only drives faster. In the wrong direction. Talking with her hands, swerving around blind curves, charging up hills. Our guests are charmed by everything. Very good at spotting hawks in the distance, not good at getting their scopes focused on them before they take off. They argue happily about species. I gave up trying to identify hawks long ago. They have too many plumages, it may take them four years to achieve their final dress. If their crowns are visible their tails are obscured by branches, and vice versa. They are as difficult as sparrows. Give me a flycatcher anytime, perched on the tip of a pole or a bare branch, darting for an insect, returning to the same spot so I can study it at rest, in profile, in flight; wings spread, wings folded. A splendid bird! A Swallow-tailed kite, now, that's easy (and lovely). Or a crimson and black tanager, although with these you must be sure where the crimson is, and where the black. Color, that's what I like in my birds, if I *must* see them in a tree. They are easier in the hand.

There are no tanagers on this trip, not in sight anyway. But the company is congenial, Dora is in top form. Finally, reluctantly, she acknowledges the hour and heads back. Speeds back. Even with me helping to balance the rear seat we bounce uncomfortably. She gives me a leer as we drive into the filling station. The man is waiting. The locals all like this friendly, crazy American. Our tire is retrieved, the gas tank filled, some tinkering goes on under the hood (as usual). We backtrack to where our weary workers stand on the roadside. Halfway home with people, poles, chairs, Dave's photographic boxes, our usual load of equipment, an upended table crowning all, we realize that the green Nova is no longer behind us. It isn't a very big car to begin with, it is in deplorable shape, it is overloaded even without a load lashed to its roof. We deposit our own carload at Parrots' Wood and dispatch a rescue team. I fill a thermos with cheer such as a St. Bernard might carry for succor, and send what cookies I can find. Dave was driving, he looked exhausted even at noon. He keeps trying to be a Machete King and it is too much for him. Later I inquire tactfully what had happened. He doesn't want to talk. He sits beside me at supper, goes off to bed. He thanks me for the thermos, though. Am I mistaken, or are we all beginning to feel that we had better get to the airport before these cars finally and forever give out? I worry about Dora, too. Some days even she looks a little as if she might give out. This afternoon was Vacation, she loved that fast driving.

Day 27

I am walking down the back road with one of my roommates at sunset looking for an owl that was seen along here at dusk yesterday. Venus is again a golden globe suspended in a golden sky. I have been reading a book on survival techniques and am trying to walk like an Indian, rolling soundlessly on the ball of my foot. Susan pounds along beside me in heavy boots, click, click, click, marching like a soldier. That is the difference between us, I think, feeling forlorn. She is forthright, four-square, knows where she is going, wastes no motion, while I wander erratically, always trying something new that will get me nowhere even if I achieve it. I am not, after all, about to go out into the wilderness to try surviving as the Indians did.

We pass the farm that lies on the far side of the Western Road, its buildings not quite square, its plantings new. The man and woman who live there are eating supper at a table outside. They wave.

"What a lonely life," Susan observes in a pitying tone. A flock of guinea hens stop talking about us and fly with a rush of wings into a pine, diverting my thoughts. Guineas are good guard birds, alert and vocal. Good eating if you can catch them, which isn't easy. They spin around in your hand, lose their feathers; you are likely to be left with a handful of pillow stuffing and no bird for supper. They are night-blind; if you can catch them in the dark they are less apt to scratch your eyes out. Give me a pelican to work with—though not to eat—any day. They came from Africa in slave ships. Guineas.

I look beyond them to fields of pineapple and coconut palm slanting down to a new citrus orchard, to the wide skies, to the hardwoods that mark the distant river. I contrast this with women in the cities going home to apartment cubicles, to silent suppers, a TV program, an occasional movie or concert or visit with relatives. No wind flowing by an open window, no rain pounding on their roofs, no flower petals (or guinea feathers) on grass, no bird songs at dawn, no crickets at dusk. This farm woman has no concerts or TV, but she has a strong man to cook for. She may have had, or will have, children. Her fire is aromatic. She has geese, hens, a dog, animals to care for. She must often be weary, but she has compensations. My companion will return to a condominium in a glamorous suburb full of glamorous shops: to golf, to a husband often away. She will have her hair and nails done. How different we are! She wouldn't understand if I said I pitied *her*. I try rolling my foot around a mud puddle where a deer left prints last night. I say—it is all I can think of to say—"I wish I had taken time to talk with that woman. She must be curious about us."

We are always so busy! I like my friend Susan. She has qualities I could wish were mine. I am just noticing the distances between people. Like the other day when a husband and wife had come to see Dora. Dora was weary, and she summoned me to backstop her. On one level the couple were compatible: long married, pleased to be a team. On another they were sharp. Opinions, even philosophies clashed, ragged edges showed, were hastily glossed over. What holds a marriage together?

After they left, Dora and I discussed this. We each had good marriages; we can speak freely. Sex in the beginning, compatibility. Then children, then habit? A safety net woven from a thousand small threads over the years until it enfolds you like a cloak that may show wear, be torn at the edges but has built a security and warmth neither is willing to discard? The shining threads of love were once the woof, maybe still are; dulled but strong. No one outside can know. What would have happened to our marriages if our men had lived? Maybe we were lucky? NO! we explode simultaneously and, laughing, go our different ways.

An hour later I was called back. This is Visitor Day. A midwestern couple, not young, wants to arrange with Diane to go caving in the mountains. We sense this is something they wish to boast about among competitive friends at home. We recognize the breed; they will pay well. I see Diane eye the woman's city shoes, the man's weight, their hands. She is not enthusiastic. Dora sees this too. Casually she asks me to fetch supplies and rebandage her instep, where her sneaker chafes on the hideous brown scar her slacks conceal. We sit at one end of the verandah, Diane transacts her business at the other, but the couple observes us. While I wind gauze Diane chats, describing a trip that might be acceptable, though there will be discomforts, the weather cannot be guaranteed. With unhappy looks at Dora and me, the couple departs, their eagerness somehow evaporated. They leave us chuckling.

"I don't need money that badly," says Diane cheerily. "Can you imagine boosting that heavy man in and out of caves?"

She goes off to see about supper. "Stew again," she warns,

also cheerily. "I can't write and think up dishes for you all at the same time. Just think how good airplane meals will taste in a few days!"

On my path I find Jaime unhappily trying to clean up his garden. A big tapir had found it in the night, appreciated the loving care Jamie gives it, had rolled about until nothing was left but mashed stems, leaves, mud, and huge footprints. Tapirs are a hazard on the highways here at night, like deer at home. They can total a car, send it rolling. That's what the men we see at sunset, walking with their guns, are hoping for (a totaled tapir, not a totaled car).

Day 28

The ladies' dormitory above me stirs early and, by the sound, starts shoving suitcases about. A few days ago dispositions had started to fray, people were giving and disputing orders. But now that we are so close to departure everyone has much still to accomplish. There are plants and scenes and leaf-cutting ants to photograph, bird songs to chase down and record, toads and butterflies to scrutinize more carefully—each is intent on her interests. The sun comes out, a breeze dispels the humidity.

The woman who wears a thermometer on her belt stops to tell me it is 68°F. at the biffy—just what I would be setting my living-room thermostat to at this hour if I were on Cape Cod. Where will I be in a few more days? With luck? A full moon pales outside the window.

I am in no hurry to dress, to face the problems the word "luck" implies. Living on the verge can grow wearing. Our cars are being used far more than was planned, are being racketed too fast over potholes. When I sit in the back seat of the station wagon that was Dora's pride when we arrived, only third-hand, "practically new," a phrase she would not use today, some mechanism under me becomes hot. Not dangerous, Dora soothes, not to worry. In the Nova the same spot is rock-hard, guaranteed to crack a coccyx. The Nova has begun to boil over every few miles, its brakes pull, it needs a constant flow of oil. Although our more conservative members—I am one—are nervous, and when we are tired tight-lipped, so far our luck has held. St. Christopher has been friendly, we have coasted half a dozen times bubbling and steaming into a bar-and-food joint properly named the Oasis, halfway between town and Parrots' Wood. The Oasis repairs and greases human as well as mechanical innards. It boasts a long counter, a few tables, country music in competition with a squawking parrot that climbs about the bars of its wooden cage, inspecting any handouts we offer. Crackers and commercial dry cookies can be obtained there, washed down by cold beer or fruit juices in lurid colors. The owner himself, JB, welcomes us—a cordial American as glad of our company as are his dogs, taking our dry, discarded cookies. Each time we linger, hoping to come back another day. We always do, of necessity.

Some attendant circumstance of our cliffhanging luck is always good for a laugh, like the other day when I was left to guard our tireless (I mean without its quota of tires) vehicle. A passing truck driver stopped, asked me to give him some gas. If our car wasn't going anywhere, why would it need gas? I didn't know if we *had* any gas; its gauge, as I've said, has never worked.

Last night, thirty-six hours before leaving time (some of us have been counting these hours), the station wagon again became temperamental.

"Just let it live until Tuesday," breathed my roommate. "Just let it get us to the airport."

It had been attended to, fed, and cosseted—again—the night before, by flashlight, by the man who had come to restore our generator to a less racketing roar. Dora and I limped it to the house of a neighbor. Neighbors aren't necessarily next door; this one was six miles distant. He is ill, Dora reported, returning from his house, but she once gave him a blood transfusion, so he is indebted. From his bed he has promised to arrive by nine in the morning. We will see.

If Dora doesn't get rid of us all soon, *she* will need a blood transfusion—a month of Life at Daily Risk is enough. Although I must say she has borne up beautifully, her hearty laugh punctuates all our hours, no crisis seems to faze her. I gave her a hug, for which she seemed grateful.

Day 29

Our nets are set a mile down our own road; we can walk to
them. At night we must take them down or guard them. I've
told you that? If you were one of those men who must spend
the night sleeping by them, fighting voracious mosquitoes,
dark falling at six, rain falling on your improvised tent, saying
it twice would hardly underscore the discomfort. But here the
road is little used; our tracks are concealed. So tonight we only
furl the nets. I volunteer to open them at dawn.

Dawn is the time of day I love most. The world is fresh,
cool, quiet, even if it is raining, which it isn't. I pocket a
banana and am off. The last I hear is a voice upstairs complaining it is COLD. I chuckle, thinking of what we are going back
home to, the raw winds, the gray skies and snows of March.
It is humid: by the time I reach our lanes I am sweating. But
I am alone, at ease. Is it wrong, I think as always, unfriendly
to like to be alone? Alone I can hear the horse in the pasture I
am passing snuffle. I can stand to watch the geese and guinea
hens feeding in the grass, trade greetings with an equally early
mockingbird on his fence post. The farmer and his woman are
already at work in their pineapple field. They wave Good
Morning.

At dusk the other night I came down this road owling. A

Ferruginous pygmy owl had been sighted, I wanted to see it. The sun had set through slits of heavy cloud. I had heard what at first I thought was a dog barking, or an owl. Then I realized it was too near for a dog and no owl I know has a breathy whoof like that. Memories! How suddenly and clearly they arrive! I was transported back to Rockbridge Alum Springs in Virginia, once a famous spa for the wealthy, in full moon on an icy October night. Silvery naked and shivering, I was running from the shower off the back porch of what had once been a slave cottage to my bed inside. I had heard this same cough, stopped, saw across the fence three deer looking at me. Surprised, no doubt, but not afraid. Laura Bailey allowed no shooting on her mountainside with its mineral springs, its elegant ballroom for 600, its covered walkways left from its glory of the 1800s. Its buildings had been designed by Stanford White, who came to a sad end.

Laura was a crack shot, the widow of two eminent ornithologists of a past generation. She had camped and canoed and climbed and cooked with them and their companions in the Everglades when these had been nothing but swamps, on mountains little explored all through the West. Chan had sent me to her, wishing to learn if there was an age differentiation between warblers I might trap and those that passed along the Maryland coast.

With difficulty I had located her wild land on a dark autumn night, led in by a U.S. forester. With a palpably false, muttered excuse he left me at the chain across her driveway to find my way to a black house. Gun in hand, Laura answered my knocking, read my note of introduction while I waited outside her door. I came to love this small, spirited woman, custodian of her deteriorated spa and the museum her husband built; her old-school formality, her cold house. Wrapped in quilts, we sat in front of her fire evenings sipping sherry while she read me letters from her father, detailing the way life had been in a past century. I wish I had those letters, any of her journals and diaries, I wish the University that may be housing them were not so distant. It was a world I would like to recreate in her memory. She would have appreciated that.

The gods of my ornithological world had been only lads when she knew them. She snorted when pridefully I brought up their names. I had to stay over an extra day once so I might tell my grandchildren I had had tea with Dr. Alexander Wetmore. (Who was he? they would ask, puzzled. Their gods are different.) We bathed on the other side of the mountain in the rundown building of an even more deteriorated spa. An aproned maid attended us, offering frilly shower caps and towels, kept a watchful guardian eye on us as we dunked and floated in her curative waters. I had to drink from Laura's seven springs. You would have to suffer badly from gout to welcome any cure their sulphur offered!

The tang of a mountain autumn with its frosted flowers, the love I came to have for this spirited lady of bygone days rushed joyfully back to me with the sound of a deer whooshing in the underbrush beside this tropical road. Would I have heard it, would the blessing of those cold, firelit evenings snug in her father's wing chair have come back to me if I had not been alone?

I guess we each have to figure out what is important to us. To me those deer, ears alert, eyes bright in the moonlight, myself poised ghostly in mid-dash are as vivid—more vivid—than that bevy of bird banders now hurrying down the road to join me at the nets. Will I be back someday hearing again a deer cough not only in Virginia but in Belize, with young pines lining my road, a pauraque calling from a puddle? It isn't a story I can easily tell, if someone asks why I went off alone.

Day 30

My roommate has a heart condition. Often in the night I wake to worry over her heavy breathing, to wonder at the curiosity and restlessness that has brought her here. But tonight I lie awake trying to dissipate a nightmare.

From the room above a woman picks her way down the stairs. Her flashlight throws monstrous shadows on the wall as she passes. My night already is full of monstrous shadows. When she returns I pull on my clothes and go out to pick my own way, on the path that leads to the Western Road with its broken pavement. I think better in motion, and I have a lot of thinking to do.

I have been lying to myself these weeks I have been here in Belize. Determined not to face truth, I have been sitting about reading, totting up figures, editing Diane's manuscript, writing bits and pieces of one of my own, baking bread. I haven't jumped eagerly out of bed each morning as for the last twenty years I have so happily done. I have explained this as the need to stand aside so others can learn, be able when I am gone to carry on the research and conservation activities that matter so much to me. I have made a big thing out of my smug generosity. It has been a fat lie.

What I am trying to cover over, what I am refusing to admit, is that I can no longer do what I wish. I no longer tell my body what to do; it is telling me. I resent this inevitable fact so much that I have been papering it over with every noble excuse I can dream up, instead of facing it. I tell myself that I have been banding birds too long, I am tired of it, I need a new career. Well, I am NOT tired of being up when the sun blazes orange through the leaves, of working outdoors until a great moon splashes white across my path, or hangs in a pendant scimitar as finally I close my nets at night. But my bones *are* weary; I *do* need a new career. So I am going to have to find one, or carve one out. Or quit.

Ever since Brad left I have said—and meant—that when I can no longer do what I want, live the way I want, I will quit. I am responsible to no one.

"Whose decision is this?" I had argued with a doctor. "This is *my* life, *my* body!" We were discussing the life-support systems that keep you technically alive when what matters to you, to your friends and family, has disintegrated.

"You haven't the right to decide to keep me alive," I sputtered at him. "Your profession is healing. You may be on a different level but basically you are like a plumber, or my clock man. You repair breaks, replace bushings, clean out pipes. You may know my physical problems, but you don't know me well enough to keep my real self, my emotional life, my spirit. If I am crippled by arthritis or Parkinson's instead of the poison ivy and sliced fingers I usually bring you, if I *want* to live I will come to you for help. When you set a shingle outside your door you were saying you would help me to the best of your ability. But if I don't want to live you haven't the right to make me. As a person, as a friend you can try to change my attitude; I'll respect that. But the decision is mine."

I hurt his ego, but doctors' egos can stand a bit of puncturing: like those of politicians and heads of corporations. They grow naturally into a sense of omnipotence, become unused to having their decisions challenged. We saw this when we lived in Washington, the changes in men and women being brought into positions of flattering importance. I worried some that Brad (he was a presidential appointee) might become affected, but he had a sturdy sense of values and was not ambitious, so not too much rubbed off on him. Our time there probably went more to my head than to his. Those long gloves I wore . . . pale blue, pale pink . . . those high heels I stood endlessly in at receptions. . . . I took my own rum with me in a drugstore bottle in my handbag. Rum was rarely served in those days, it is the only liquor I can drink without unhappy effects. I don't drink much of it, either—just talk (or write) about it: but if you are going to survive night after night of Washington receptions you need assistance. I look on a drink as a medical relaxant, very useful at a party where I know no one, at a dinner table set with a formidable array of silver and food I don't need.

Long gloves and rum haven't much to do with my discussions with doctors—which haven't much to do with the group's discussion at the moment of how best to put to use our time tomorrow morning. Half of us are going to go in one direction, half in another.

That night I revive the subject in the upstairs dormitory. We are propped on the beds: a doctor's wife, protective of his profession; a woman recuperating from a major operation, well aware of the valley of the shadow of death; my roommate, with the bad heart, of whom the same must be true; and two younger women, who don't yet want to look at the fact and possible discomfort of dying. It makes for a lively discussion, not resolved.

Knowing I can quit has been a comfort to me. Several times I have seriously considered it but delayed, been grateful as new adventures, new people, new twists to living unexpectedly surfaced. (I suspect I have also delayed because I lack the character to get my scattered affairs in order.) If the decision were clean-cut there would be no problem. My life is my own, to live as I wish, to dispose of when I wish. But is it? Or have I painted myself into a corner?

Yesterday when I walked past the pineapple farm with its guinea hens I had stopped and talked with the woman there, interested in her life, in the robust attitude she showed toward it. This is what I have done these years I have been alone— worked myself into other people's lives for my own selfish reasons, to keep myself going. Until, even if I didn't mean to, didn't realize what was happening, deliberately I acquired an extended family scattered from California to Florida, from Louisiana to Maine. I have made myself into a surrogate grandmother, a friendly aunt or cousin to whom its members may come—this year, next year, sometimes it is long before they surface—for comfort and care; to borrow money, to be spoiled for a few days; to be loved. In need of someone who will listen (and try not to advise). They *do* surface. They pay me back royally in filling my loneliness, in giving *me* comfort and care and spoiling, letting me borrow warmth from their lives.

So now, because my knees are old, I no longer see or hear as well as I did, my fingers have grown gnarled, I am bored and discouraged, I should turn on them? Say, in essence, "You have been useful, thanks. But the humiliations of age are more important to me than our friendship, I am quitting"?

Can I callously withdraw like that, reject them, let them know I never really cared about their concerns? We learn to lose our friends. Rejection is something other. Am I so badly off that I can deliberately do this? I love these people, or at the least I respect and am fond of them. I worked my own way into our friendships. And like love, friendship carries obligations. My father wove that into my childhood, made it a tenet of my philosophy.

Or is this false pride, and I am fooling myself again? Making another excuse because death is final and who knows what tomorrow might bring? Where does truth lie? How do we know what motives really control us? Why do the elderly and ill keep on living, clutching at life? Out of fear? Curiosity? The happy ones are rare. I have to decide, to think hard about all this. Unwilling to face up to how my next few years (if I have any coming) must be handled, is why I have been complaining here all month about the climate, the mud, the lack of fresh adventure. I have been morose, critical instead of merry, surly: have lost myself. Perhaps the others have been too busy to notice. I have a few days left to make up. I don't need to be so down in the dumps; you choose your paths in this world. Well, I'm not sure about this, but at least you can try . . .

Across a field the sky is lightening. It is time I turned back.

"This is another day," Hal Borland wrote in one of his seasonal diaries I treasure. "Another blank page in the endless book of time, another chance . . ." I italicize those last two words. If the road of the spirit as well as of the land I have been picking my way over is uneven and fissured, so are all our roads. If we are fortunate we have flashlights to guide us, our feet are supple, puddles are to jump. You can even, if you practice long enough, learn to walk like an Indian.

Somewhere ahead of me—in my mail at home, in a chance remark by an acquaintance, perhaps even from that manuscript in New York, will come a shift in my life, a new direction to follow. Adventure, I remind myself, thanking Archie, is a state of mind.

I should be ashamed of myself. I am, but now I am cheerful about it. I roll on my instep around a puddle. Time, I tell myself later in the morning, Time is what we all need and most of us don't take it. Time to read, to think, to grow.

I have recaptured my serenity. With departure imminent, a lot of recapitulation and merry talk has been going on. I have been thanked, and genuinely, for my contribution to the project—not for that staff of life, the bread loaves, but for the staffs of knowledge and helpfulness. I find this embarrassing but of course gratifying. So my bouts of self-pity haven't been as apparent as I feared, everyone has been preoccupied with their own concerns and self-doubts. It is only reasonable that I should be slowing down. Our table even listened to, and laughed at stories I got into telling at breakfast. Maybe I haven't lost myself after all. Or am refound. Everyone's life is filled with ups and downs.

Time. Together we compete—to tell a story, report a longer list, go back to the buffet for another helping before someone else gets it. The urge to better our neighbor, to parade our own interests and experiences, is universal (probably why some people write journals).

This morning I am alone, relaxed now that I have come to terms with myself, have figured out why my weeks here have been negative. It is our last full day. The cars left for some special birdwatching mecca after breakfast. Maria has cleaned the kitchen, scrubbed the verandah, and left, trusting me and the dogs. Maria has her own home, with the demands of eight children.

Two other women also stayed behind, but they have disappeared to pursue their own interests. If they were here we would have to chat. I would be straining that darned deaf ear of mine to hear what they said, would have to hold up my social end. Instead, now the dishpan with the last of our bran and oats and yeast is filled with dough and set to rise, the Dobermans are reassured that they are loved, I settle on the verandah and watch martins swoop and circle over the pond. They are hungry after yesterday's bad weather. I might fetch Diane's typewriter from her room, but I am enjoying Time. I want to do nothing.

By chance I pick up a book by a man who recounts how one he wrote earlier, unexpectedly successful, has enabled him to do what he really wants with his life. It is a joyful book of a man come alive. It sets me to ruminating on what I want to do with the time left to me. I consider this as I punch down my bread dough, feel it spring under my palms, roll it into loaves. I am impelled by no ambition, the day is not a set of empty hours to be filled with accomplishments.

All morning I have felt myself growing. My tree is sending out new shoots. Its buds are not yet uncurled, they may not make it to leaf and blossom, to wide branches offering shade, but who is to say? I can only wait, pleasurably aware of the stir of sap.

I'll be glad to go home; this climate saps my energy. It is true I have been banding birds for too many years. It is time for me to take another road. Thirty years is a generation; I need regeneration. What motivates me is challenge, something new to deal with, the nervousness that comes from feeling inadequate, the learning, the triumph when something succeeds, the people who teach me, the new friends. Even when I can't do a job well it leads to something else; another door opens. My past is strewn with attempts—and fun.

I will return to a carapace I had built to store my books and records, pots and pans and paintings, furniture that came to Boston in sailing ships, which I should take better care of for my grandchildren. When I unlock my door that house will be

empty, cold. And quiet—so quiet. . . . Those first minutes I
will stand, my heart constricted, crying WHAT AM I DOING
HERE? There is no place, no one to run to for comfort. I have
a sister with imagination. When I still lived in Washington,
in the Georgetown row home where Brad and I had been
together, whenever I returned from a trip she would have a
bowl of flowers on my—our—hall table; something alive,
glowing to welcome me, speaking of love. The house on Cape
Cod is silent, although from the pines a chickadee will pipe
an inquiry at my presence.

Brad is not in this house I had built. He is a photograph, a
citation on the wall. Because you cannot see wind, the sun's
energy that lies in golden light upon the grass, does this mean
these don't enfold us? It is odd that he has come back to me
so rarely in all these years—he himself, his hand closed on
mine. Once I was lying on a hospital cart, awaiting a verdict
from men who moved about me. Once I had fallen from a
boat, was treading water. Once . . . I was at my desk in firelight, my head in my hands. For a long moment his shoulder
comforted me, my panic subsided. Then slowly, like the ghosts
in stories—

"Don't go!" I had cried wildly. He was wearing a bathrobe
his grandson-namesake now takes from the closet when he comes
to visit. "DON'T GO!" My voice had strangled in nightmare.
He was gone. Death I can accept; there is no choice. Absence
is something else.

My parents, now—it's funny about my parents. They show
up every so often, unsummoned. Memory can bring my mother
to my bed at night to rub growing pains from my knees, bring
my father's voice as he lifts me to his shoulder. But when they
come unbidden it is as if they had just come to call, were just
stopping by to see how I am doing. They have not come to

give me support. It is as if they are assaying me. They have come to remind me that I am only a ring in the chain that links children whose photographs are on my table to their forebears whom I know only from history books—a doctor who attended George Washington, first Dean of the Faculty of Medicine at Columbia College. His genes must have reached me—he arranged for a botanical garden of medicinal herbs to be planted about his hospital. History does not comment on any of the women in our chain. My grandmothers I knew only briefly. One was small and severe. Her rustling skirts could frighten me, but she played cards with me before my early bedtime; there was love between us. The other spent her visits to us tatting and taciturn. Pushed to one side and unhappy, I realize now, in a household busy with undisciplined children, dogs, confusion. I remember her most clearly—and savagely—for the day she held me while my mother whacked me with a hairbrush for disobedience. What tag-ends surface from our lives; what a legacy to leave!

Do my parents appear to test the strength of my link, to assess any weakening? Will I someday also be a shadowy presence to that babe I wrote of, gurgling in her mother's backpack? Will I appear to assess her strength? Who knows? Some of my grandchildren I know well, some not, but we share our blood. I am a part of their history, I must stand tall for them. And for those who have generously befriended me these past years.

I sigh. It isn't easy to stand tall, to be trusted. Love is soft. You give it joyfully. It can come and go. Trust—that's harder. You have to earn it. It is a flame that must be guarded. Once extinguished it cannot be relit.

You are never alone in the world. So it behooves you— me—to keep my chin lifted, my honor clear, my floors dusted.

When my time comes to die it will come. (I suppose that in spite of all those angry words I snarled that day at my doctor, it is not for me to hasten or to manage.) I am not sure I accept this, but I seem to be living by it.

Across the verandah I see Steve watching me. He knows I am far away. He came up the stairs a few minutes ago, settled quietly with his own book. We didn't need to speak. We don't see each other often, we live too distant to work together, but there is understanding between us, a solid relationship. What will he go back to? His marital life is not easy. He has passed often through that door I will unlock on Cape Cod. He is there inside, as well as here across the verandah.

For I will go home to that house I built. The door will stick, as usual, need the pressure of my knee. It will be, as I said, cold and silent inside. Then, as I hang up my coat, bring in my luggage, slowly my house will come alive. It is the people who have entered, the people who have been happy there, who make a home out of whatever shelter you have, be it a house, a tent, a van, a boat. If they are fond of you, they leave a piece of their heart behind, an ambience, a ghost of spirit at ease. My heart—fortunately it seems to regenerate—is scattered all up and down the Atlantic from Trinidad to Hilton Head; to a Jersey marsh, to Vermont, to Maine. A piece of it is in an Adirondack boathouse, in rooms looking out on Pacific surf, on a Kentucky crabapple tree, on an Arizona desert. You will find me at the window of a New York apartment where finches peck at a frozen winter windowbox. I walk into these rooms as into happiness, knowing I am welcome, belong. As these people in my home belong.

This isn't memory. Some of my visitors I have never met— they were here in my absence, knowing which rock the key lives under. Here a child is curled up in the big chair by the fireplace, his book open beside it. On the bathroom shelf is a lipstick left by an unknown woman: pretty, my neighbor reported. Someone is brewing coffee in the kitchen. To them too this house has been a home, and now, when I need them, they are here, like bright sparks from the fire I light. Someone has built me a fire to light, knowing I would be cold, need the cheerful blaze to warm my spirit as well as my hands.

"When I look around," wrote a man, leaving his thanks with the key "in an odd way it is as if you are here." He sounded surprised.

But of course I am here, it isn't odd at all. And now, to my pleasure I am aware of him looking into the fridge, mending the troublesome lock on my door: his hand is on my telephone. The ghosts of those who have crossed my threshold wrap me in cloaks of many textures. Their voices speak in my cold rooms.

I often wonder about the homes where we have lived. Surely at times their present occupants must hear my step in their bedrooms, our children running through the halls? See my flowers blooming on their windowsills, hear my music sounding from the walls? As I am aware here in Diane's home of a younger woman, not Diane, moving about our bedroom, amused by its dormitory arrangement, touching the plants we tend for her. Shadows from the leaves outside play on her skirt. She is as aware of me, reading on my bed, as I am of her. We are, somehow, kin.

People give me worried looks when I talk like this. Why is it queer? Chan hears bird notes none of us do. Musicians play symphonies and sonatas in their heads, tea and wine tasters use senses you and I lack or have never refined. The Dobermans tell us when other animals come into the compound. Can't you easily go back to a scene where you were among friends, smell perfume, pipe smoke drifting in the air of years ago? My mother had strong extrasensory perceptions, I can't compare with her. But I often know—if my senses are open—who is on the other end of my telephone, whose letter is lying on my hall floor below the postman's slot. There is a letter there now of importance; I can see part of it clearly, slipped out between junk mail. Will it be one that will trigger my future, once I am home?

The world is full of currents we can't lay corporeal hands on—trust, faith, gravity, magnetic fields, love. (Where is that list of Dorothy Gilman's back on page 13?) They add richness to all our hours. Even if, as scoffers warn me, I am as often wrong as right. I don't mind scoffers. They must have something that sustains them equally. I just wish they would be willing to tell me, so I might tune in on their frequencies too.

I wonder about that letter, seeing it again on the rug of my hall. I never have to plan What To Do. Life picks me up by the scruff of my neck, not always gently. But I need a future to look forward to, to bring that glint of adventure to my eye.

There must be someone who can use me, I think, as I wash my mixing bowl and clean the mahogany table for the last time. In spite of my creaking joints. I am cheerful. I am willing—if not eager—to mend bird nets. I am an excellent packer of luggage into cars, a good bread baker, good at picking up what has been left behind. I like people and will usually do as I am told. (Usually. I also have a full quota of faults, but I prefer not to list these.) While I talk a lot about being adventurous, there has always been someone on my ventures to run the jeeps and boats, repair temperamental equipment, clean the fish, do my arithmetic.

I will leave a piece of my heart here at Parrots' Wood. Where? By the pond? In my corner of the Common Room, coffee drinkers chatting around me, a pile of unclaimed laundry under my arm?

The martins have left my slice of sky. Those two women are

at the gate, a walk having sharpened their appetites, no doubt. I am in charge of lunch—bananas and cheese and the last of the peanut butter. My bread is ready to bake, which means another argument with that oven, seated on the floor, my leg propping the door open, my thumb aching on the button until the balky mechanism decides to function. Diane is better at this than I.

In my desk drawer at home, faded and thumbed, is a quotation from Sigurd F. Olson I copied, I don't know from where, twenty years ago. I was looking for a way to live. His reach toward the future, the road he set me on, seems as good a way to end this journal as any.

> Life is a series of open horizons, with one no sooner completed than another looms ahead. . . . Penetrations into the unknown, all give meaning to what has gone before and courage for what is to come. More than physical features they are horizons of mind and spirit. . . . And when there are no longer any beckoning mirages ahead a man dies.